From deficiency &

5 Essential
Principles For Healing
BLACK MEN
And Raising
BLACK BOYS

By

KASIM ABDUR RAZZAQ
CEO/Psychotherapist/Consultant
Abdur Razzaq Counseling & Social Architecture, PA

www.razzaqcounseling.com

www.kasimabdurrazzaq.com

*~Kasim is by far one of the most crafted and thoughtful
minds I have ever met.*
~S.B.

*~Kasim is a man before his time. He has blazed a trail for
young black men.*
~R.D.B.

From deficiency & excess to balance

ISBN-13: 978-1718717299
ISBN-10: 1718717296

A Message To The Reader

The content of this book was written using a deductive process. That is to say, each chapter identifies a *principle* or general concept, which is examined through premise and personal anecdote. Conversely, the *principles* or general concepts identified within this writing are the result of an inductive process. Meaning each *principle* in this book is a theoretical explanation of the pattern observed from *Self-study* (working as a psychotherapist in our community). Therefore, it is relevant for the reader to discern that successful navigation of this book demands you connect your personal experiences to the principles. This allows the principles to be personalized and offers unique insight and solution to each individual reader. This is the wisdom of Afrikan story telling. To allow each person to find their own specific (solution) meaning in the architecture of a shared story. This is collective self-determination, a hidden principle for those with understanding!

Dedication

It is with honor and love that I dedicate this writing to my ancestors who live through me and in me. I offer these words and experiences to black people all over the world who are in need of healing and desire healthy families and healthy communities. I write this book standing on the shoulders of every Afrikan scholar that made it their business and thought it valuable to scribe the experiences of black people. A special thank you to every person and family from the Afrikan diaspora that entrusted me with the honor of serving them, listening to their stories and mining the jewels from our collective experience. You are a huge reason that this book exists. As you have allowed me to learn, heal, and grow, I offer you this book as a means of reciprocation and fostering healthy circuitry that you may in return learn, heal, and grow.

I dedicate this work to my family and community that has poured abundantly into me their time, talent, wisdom, finances, love, and trust. This book is a trust and commitment to my hopes and inspirations (Rayyan, Isa, and Mahdi). Mostly this book is dedicated to a woman of great exception, my emotional guide, my complement and loving wife, Tinaisha Abdur Razzaq.

Today we have contributed to the social theory necessary for black people to survive, heal, and thrive. And we have developed this masterpiece through self-study, a subject to subject relationship, not pathological experimentation or

4

research conducted as a subject to object encounter. We have acted with one another instead of being acted upon, therefore, the product is self-love and healing.

To my black people with love, honor, and reverence,

The Architect

Table of Contents

Introduction

The time has come for black people to be free; free from dis-ease, sickness, pathology, and incomplete personhood. It is time for healing; healing from injustice and inhumanity. This is a call to Afrikan men, a trust to Afrikan women, a commitment to Afrikan children, and a response to devastated Afrikan families and communities. We must pronounce as Afrikan men that we are here and committed to healing and to resolving our historical and intergenerational traumas so that we can stand tall, proud, and complete for those in need of our full cosmic energy as well as for ourselves and those that have preceded us.

Black men, in our debilitated condition, we have languished in a traumatized comatose state and neglectful of our responsibility to the world. Well, I'm here to inform you that trauma is a power dynamic and healing is a power dynamic. And if you want to heal from BLACK trauma, you are going to need BLACK POWER! We are engaging our healing from a position of strength, hope, and abundance not deficit, weakness nor popularized belief. I mean we are going to take a look inside for answers not to be dependent on external sources for a resolution to our dis-ease. If you want to know about a panther, it is only logical to ask a panther, not a coyote nor a hyena. This is a study of the panther by the panther. And we can only accept the panther's perspective for our healing! As the sage, John Henrik Clarke stated, *"The ideology of our former slave masters cannot save us. We will not be truly liberated until we become the main instrument and the liberation that I am mainly concerned with is the liberation of our minds being dependent on other people to do our thinking."*

For more than two decades, I have been in a process of self-study. A study of my personal experience, a study of the young Afrikan boys I have served, a study of the Afrikan men that I have served, a study of the Afrikan men in my family, and a study of our Afrikan elders. It is my intention to share the powerful experiences, wisdoms, pain, and triumph with the community as has been the cultural practice of Afrikan people from generation to generation. I hope that my words remind those that like to be reminded, those that like not to be reminded, and inform those that don't know. Additionally, I encourage black men to explore this book and its concepts with black women, boys, and girls to activate a spirit of togetherness. Most importantly, my aim of this writing is to highlight the importance and initiate the revitalization of healthy Afrikan families and communities so that we may experience collective healing. That being said, I testify that there is no healing of the Afrikan man without healing the Afrikan woman (as well as our Afrikan children). Our healing is collectively interconnected and interdependent as our wholeness is interdependent and interconnected. It is only our vain desires, narcissism, lack of commitment, and flight from responsibility that we (black men) imagine being healed without having healed black women (or black children). And it is the eradication of this very state of mind and arrested spiritual development that we are battling against. As we move from dis-ease to healing, as black men we must first make the psychological shift from *I to We.*

Afrikan men, it is time to transform our trauma to triumph. On this journey, we have to leave behind our parachutes and safety nets and work with full commitment that we will either heal or die. We cannot be tentative nor waiver on this decision as our humanity is contingent upon its resolve.

Healing

"I come from nothing, and I come from everything." ~ Kasim age 15
(Interpreted to mean I didn't have much growing up but I had family &
community, so I always had everything I needed)

To heal is to return to our natural state. Healing acknowledges a disturbance from a healthy state of being, typically demarcated by pain, hurt, and discomfort. Therefore, in order to heal or to return to our natural state, we must intentionally and strategically revisit the elements of pain and hurt using *conscious discomfort.* Conscious discomfort is the planned and purposeful process of experiencing pain to both heal and grow. Healing is an intrapersonal process; it does not happen to a thing, rather, it happens within the thing. And because healing happens from within, it is necessary to have *sacred space* to foster the process. A space that accepts personal expertise and builds capacity to heal internally. A space that cultivates healthy regeneration and fosters restoration.

The work of healing is not exclusive to the poor, undereducated or those lacking social status. The work of healing is inclusive of anyone exemplifying cultural imbalance. Therefore, contrary to popular perception, acquired assets, earned titles, authority, and social status do not recuse anyone from imbalanced wellbeing. Just as lack of resource, marginalization, and feeble finances do not designate dis-ease or imbalance. I testify to these understandings as they are evidenced daily through social media, news outlets, and personal anecdotes of the wealthy and famous suffering from imbalance and dis-ease despite

11

their riches and celebrity. Hardship is not an indicator of imbalance and wealth is not indicative of health. We must strive to achieve cultural wholeness as Afrikan men no matter our current station in life. We must return to our natural state so that we may live out our collective purpose instead of our individualized desires.

Healing is happening all around us, all the time, yet we pay it very little attention or undermine its (present moment) phenomena by placing value only on finality (product versus process). However, to observe nature is to have correct understanding of the healing process. You have seen it before or maybe even experienced it yourself. Take for example when I was 11 years old and broke my foot playing football at the rec center. My brother carried me home that day because I couldn't walk. I was pretty sure my foot was broken. A few hours later, my intuition was confirmed as the doctor read the results of the CT scan. The doctor was able to show me exactly where the break occurred. He let me know the foot would have to be reset in order to heal properly. The doctor was responsible for identifying the break, resetting my foot, and casting the injured area. After that, he let me know his job was done. He said, "Now you just have to give it time to heal." This doctor with all his education, tools, machines, technology, and expertise could not heal my foot. He affirmed the truth, that I was the expert and technology responsible for my healing. Afrikan healing is about reconnecting to a spirit of *self-determination.* I sat for three weeks experiencing discomfort, my foot firmly secured in its *sacred space* (a cast). After a little under a month, my cast was taken off and I had complete use of my fully healed foot. For those three weeks, all I cared about or thought about was when my foot would be healed. I wanted the cast off my foot so I could play football again. In the weeks that I was healing, I never attended football practice. I felt unworthy and unimportant to the team unless I was healed and could perform my job as a running back. I had placed product over process, and in doing so, I lost valuable moments waiting on the future.

The persistent and continued dehumanization and trauma inflicted upon Afrikan people throughout the world using racism, imperialism, experimentation, deception, and colonization is correctly referred to as *Maafa*. Maafa is a Kiswahili word meaning great disaster. Our revered scholar Dr. Marimba Ani has offered us this Afrikan word to define Afrikan phenomena! She informs us that, *"We are using the word to reclaim our right to tell our own story. Because Maafa has disconnected us from our cultural origins we have remained vulnerable in a social order that does not reflect our cultural identity."* The overarching consequence of this experience has been fragmentation and incomplete personhood, which has rendered Afrikan people (Black men particularly) in an unnatural and imbalanced state. Therefore, an urgent call has been placed upon Afrikan men to begin our process of restoration and healing. As we respond to this call, we have to affirm and stay connected to our mission of *healing*. This means that we have to value process and remain in the present moment. We must celebrate our healing as well as continue our journey toward being healed. We will not allow internal or external stimuli to devalue our process and place shame or guilt upon our personhood as we are becoming. So Black men, what are we healing from? How are we defining our current state of being and where are we returning? I suggest that we are healing from **Psycho-cultural imbalance**. That is to say that our thinking and actions are ill-aligned with our cultural values resulting in psycho-cultural dis-ease and imbalance. Therefore, we must return to **Psycho-cultural equilibrium**. That being a state of thinking and behaving that is in the best interest of Afrikan people demonstrating alignment and adherence to collective and communal values. Afrikan brothers, it is our time to live whole, complete, and with cultural balance celebrating process and product. We are worthy, important, and capable right NOW! Let us act with urgency, diligence, commitment, and being gentle with ourselves. Our healing is long overdue and has left us, our (Afrikan women) complements and our (Afrikan children) legacy are in a devastated condition. We can no longer allow ourselves permission to continue the destruction caused from living as unnatural, incomplete human beings.

My intention with this writing is to reflect on my personal process of abandoning dis-ease, fragmentation, and incomplete personhood with the goal of undergoing an intensive healing transformation. My journey of returning to a natural state, a restored state of humanity and harmony within myself, family, and the community has been complete with challenges, setbacks, vulnerability, pain, success, theoretical as well practical wisdom. The journey is far from over, however, in this present moment I have reached a space of clarity and strength that has compelled me to (externalize) impregnate the minds and hearts of others with my seeds of experience. I have come to embrace this natural male process of internalization followed by externalization for the purpose of creating life, and in it, I have found restoration. More importantly, I have gained insight into healing.

In my practice as a psychotherapist, people come in for support after experiencing hurt. And their hope is to leave healed. As a matter of fact, a common question that people ask is *When will I be fixed?* This is a question that usually happens after the person has reported their history of pain and trauma. This writing is important because of the content but more so because of its timing. Most people wait until they have completed something to discuss the final product or celebrate its culmination. Through this process of *self* study, I have gained insightful consciousness and understanding of true healing. We are stuck in our past and waiting on the future. Well, what happens in between? Healing! Healing, happens in between! I testify that healing is a present tense experience. This writing is most important because healing is happening as I'm typing these pages. I'm not healed. I'm in process, the process of healing. In order to be healed, we have to bring ourselves into a conscious state of acceptance for the present moment and our healthy actions being implemented. I learned the context of healing and present moment experience while serving clients. I witnessed clients devastated by their past and hoping in the future to be completely *over it or through it.* They were waiting to be healed. As I noticed the transformation in clients, which often eluded them or was minimized by them, I began to understand my role in helping them to see their healing in the present moment.

It should be understood throughout this reading that *self* as we discuss the black man is not entirely nor exclusively speaking to the individual but is a reference to the cultural understanding of *self* as the individual and the collective. That is to say, the healing of black men is interconnected and interdependent with the healing of black women, our immediate families, and the black community at large. This understanding is affirmation and alignment with our cultural thinking and behavior captured in the wise words *I am because we are*. The fragmentation and violation of the personhood of Black men is a social, economic, and political strategy of our oppressors that demand we remain in a state of dis-ease. In order for us black men to begin our healing process, we must first accept as truth that others benefit from our being fragmented and that our healing poses an immediate threat and end to those benefits. This form of understanding is a political consciousness that refines the focus, the aim, and the behavior of Afrikan men. However, it is necessary that this political awakening reside both in the minds and the hearts of black men. The healing of Afrikan brothers is contingent upon harmony and ongoing reconciliation between our hearts and our minds. We are not exclusively rational beings devoid of feeling nor entirely emotional deprived of executive functioning. Instead, we are complete human beings with both masculine and feminine energy meant to intermingle and provide balance so that our thoughts, feelings, and actions produce justice. Black men let this fundamental concept of politicization and *self*-action be understood and lived that our healing may be expedited.

Culture

One of the most detrimental practices of the black community has been the failure to accept and teach a political definition of culture by which we can live, unite, and become free. For black people to know their culture, we must have a politically effective definition for it. We must have a definition that helps us to focus our attention on concepts that facilitate sovereignty and complete personhood for every black life. If black people intend to be healthy and free, we have to understand and operate under the definition that our beloved mother and elder Dr. Marimba Ani gave which is, *"Culture is our immune system!"* How befitting and astute her analogy becomes when we contemplate the physical genocide being carried out on our black bodies through death-producing *"gut health"* practices. Black people all across the nation have adopted eating and drinking (highest consumer of sugary drinks) habits that are destroying our physical vessels. I remember talking to a college friend of mine (Dr. Jason Scott Holly) who informed me that 90% of health conditions impacting the black community are directly related to our diet. There are likely many positions and responses (food desserts, finances, knowledge, etc.) to the quandary of the black diet and why we destroy our bodies through our food CHOICES! However, the WHY and SOLUTION is just that, our diet is a function of choice! And choice is a function of cognition, attitudes, beliefs, and values, therefore, addressing the physical condition of the black community is still a matter of *"Taking hold of the black mind."* As you see, there is an interconnectedness between the sickness that has pervaded the mind, body, and spirit of black people. In order to regain the balance of this trilateral union, it is vital that we become culturally activated. The Afrikan body is under constant emotional, psychological, chemical, and physical attack. Let us understand that our culture is responsible for protecting our Afrikan bodies, not the police, schools, hospitals or any other institutional entity that has an investment in seeing us dead. I'm talking about social death, emotional death, psychological death, and physical death. Because many of us are so far removed from the political action embedded within our culture, we are nothing more than the *walking dead,* departed from culture thus removed from living.

Culture, just as our immune system functions as a wellness and protective system for black people. Our culture protects us from foreign invaders that intend to weaken, create illness or destroy us. Culture is well acquainted with the needs of our trilateral system (Mind, body, spirit). In fact, our culture is so familiar that it immediately picks up on and tries to get rid of anything (thoughts, behavior, and emotional dispositions) unbeneficial. Black culture like all other cultures is politically charged and informed. That is to say, black culture insists on concerning itself with the political interests of *self* (Black interests). Every nation was given a culture, a way of living, a way of understanding and protecting itself. Similar to the uniqueness of the tissues, organs, and cells that comprise our immune system, so does each nation have its own particular cultural traditions (behaviors), beliefs (ways of understanding), attitudes (emotional disposition), and values. Every nuanced detail is deliberate, purposeful, and interconnected to the larger (trilateral) system. In order to have an optimal functioning immune system, it is necessary that all of its components be present and working cooperatively. These are the politics of self-empowerment, self-determination, sovereignty, and self-preservation. As for culture, in order to have an optimal cultural functioning, black people must possess and demonstrate these exact political tenets with our minds, bodies, and spirits. This being the case, it can be said that all (psychological, emotional, and spiritual) sickness experienced by black people are induced by deficiency or imbalance in living out our cultural worldview. To be very specific, Afrikan people become sick by either not knowing their culture (cognition), acting against their culture (behavior), adopting foreign culture (cognition and behavior) or through unilateral oversaturation of cultural aspects (cultural imbalance). Culture is our immune system! To be culturally imbalanced or work against our cultural interest means without a doubt to be sick. This sickness is not our predestined state but rather a consequence of *Cultural departure*! Therefore, healing and wellness for Afrikan people can only occur through political assertiveness and cultural adherence.

If we are going to take hold of our black minds, we have to regain sufficient knowledge of our culture and embrace a process that works to the interests (politics) of our culture. The definition we have chosen for culture provides a sufficient rubric for determining what is within our cultural purview and what is "foreign." The immune system has one function, life production. It protects our life, creates optimal conditions to sustain our life, and secures a pathway for our life to be continued. Therefore, culture is all things life-producing, life-sustaining, and life-protecting that function in the best interest of the *Self*. If black people use this basic and simple rubric to contemplate, identify, and activate cultural components, rule out unfamiliarity and destroy "dis-ease," we will return to our position of greatness and sovereignty. These actions constitute an intra-psychological revolution by black people to take hold of our Afrikan minds!

The Beginning/The End

I was born anew this year; my life began fresh like the sprouting of flowers and leaves in the coming of spring time after a long winter season covered with stillness, darkness sitting in the rich fertile soil. Despite many accomplishments, accolades, and milestones achieved throughout my life, it wasn't until this year (My 38th year on this planet) that I was able to shift out of experiencing life from a *trauma worldview*. Trauma is about surviving not living. For the first time at 38 years old, I left out of the country. For the first time at 38 years old, I took a true vacation for myself. For the first time at 38 years old, I took the risk to invest 100 percent in myself. For the first time at 38 years old, I made my complete health a top priority. For the first time at 38 years old, I decided to walk away from the safety of being a full time employee and instead work full time as a business owner. For the first time at 38 years old, I wrote a book detailing my life experiences and shared it with the world.

At 38 years old my life is beginning, my children and my wife are seeing a new version of me. Thirty-eight is a special year; it is a year of beginnings and ends. I never imagined life after thirty-eight years of age. I never planned for life after thirty-eight years of age. And I have always carried an eerie feeling from the age of nineteen that I would die when I was thirty-eight. For nineteen years I have carried, struggled, and lived with the heavy spiritual/emotional weight of believing that end of life was in close grasp for me. Why? Why have I carried and lived with this traumatic worldview? Why the age 38? Well, when I was nineteen years old, my father died in our living room at the very young age of 38.

I was there that night in my room right off the living room studying for a college class. I could hear the tv on in the living room, lights off and only the glare from the tv's picture illuminating the room. I remember my oldest brother walking in the front door, saying, "As salaam alaikum" with no response. My brother continued to my room and said, "What's up with your dad, he's not speaking to people?" I replied, "I don't know, he been in there like that all night." Only a few seconds later, I heard a scream, "Kas!" I jumped from my desk responding to my brother's voice, the lights fully on in the living room now. My brother lifted our father's body from the couch by his clothes with a possessed strength and yelled "Kas, call 911!" My body calm, voice monotone, 911- "What's your emergency?" Me- "I need an ambulance to…" My brother- "Kas, he's dead!" I responded on the call "Never mind, he's dead." I hung up the phone. My brother, a person that I revered for his toughness and looked to for physical strength was devastated and overcome with emotion. My youngest sister and brother hearing the screams came running down the stairs to find out what was going on. I stopped them at the top of the stairs and ordered them back into their rooms. I covered my brother with the strongest embrace as he fell into my arms in the middle of the room. I couldn't cry, I couldn't scream and for several months I still couldn't. I only felt the emotional sensations that accompany experiencing finality. At thirty-eight years old my father's life (his story) ended and nineteen years later at the age of thirty-eight I am beginning my life by ending my trauma story and emerging from sacred space with a healed and restored worldview.

Consciousness of the Creator

Afrikan boys and Afrikan men living as healthy whole human beings possess an intellectual and spiritual understanding of the universal law. These are the laws of equality, justice, balance, and complement. This lesson in universal harmony can be learned through the dynamic of creator and creation. Afrikan boys have to be trained in the understanding that they are part of creation, existing as a *unique* yet *integral* part of all creation. To understand their uniqueness means to study, identify, and live out the specific characteristics of self. To comprehend that they are integral dictates they understand, prioritize, and utilize their uniqueness in complement and harmony with the rest of creation. These concepts are contrary to the popularized explicit and implicit psycho-social-emotional orientation of black boys.

Our Afrikan boys have been reared in the mindset of modern-day oppressors as a result of the dis-ease carried forward by their fathers. Black boys have a dichotomous and hierarchical understanding of male/female, man/woman that has warped their understanding of self and relationship to all other creation. The psychology of many of our Afrikan boys has positioned them as the center of the world, self-absorbed, and with delusional cognitions that they are top of all creation or even worse the creator from which all other life is created. It is easy to find this psychological grooming within the literature, oral stories, and social concepts that many of our black boys are exposed too early in life. These social constructs have left our boys and men in a state of imbalance void of true consciousness of the creator and their relationship with Afrikan women.

To be conscious of the creator is to have an absolute understanding that all of creation is designed to work in harmony as an essential component that comprises a system of balance. Therefore, the healing or restoration of Afrikan men and healthy raising of Afrikan boys is contingent upon implementation of this wisdom. A black boy that is not raised to work "with" people is destined to be a black man that works "on" people. As we train our Afrikan boys in our homes, we have to impart the spirit of harmony, collaboration, togetherness, and interdependence with his siblings, mother, father, and other family relations. As we recover and heal from our dis-ease (patriarchy, colonized mind) as Afrikan men, we have to model exactly what this spiritual connectedness looks like.

In my fifteen years of marriage to an Afrikan woman, I have observed myself carry out psychological sickness and dis-ease through self-centered behavior. I was a *me monster*. Everything was about me, how it was affecting me, what benefit it could have for me, why me, and things are great because of me. I was very much in a state of ego excess and disconnected from my intended relationship with the rest of creation particularly my complement. Even the sweetest of tone and most subtle of advice could not penetrate my megalomania. My wife would say to me *I just need you to be nice to me.* Translation *get yourself together, understand what it means to be a partner and stop your narcissism before I bring you back into reality the HARD WAY.* Well, I have to tell you I'm hard-headed. Yes, she brought me back *the HARD WAY.* Trust me, I don't plan on taking that route again! However, it is the love and spiritual connectedness to the creator that resides within my Afrikan wife that informs her mystic wisdom. I am learning to appreciate and revere the unique qualities of my black wife as I heal and find balance. Additionally, I am learning to generalize this understanding and practice of complement with my Afrikan daughter, black women in my family and black women in my community. It feels amazing and whole to have a proper understanding, relationship, and work in harmony as a part of creation instead of *acting out* and against in a state of deficiency and excess. Along my journey of restoration, I began to train myself with some basic practices. These practices are the five essential principles of healing black men and raising black boys. I offer these wisdoms to Afrikan people that we may resolve our past and achieve our full potential in the future through healthy actions in our present!

PRINCIPLE I
Mastering our appetites

"I'm in shark mode." ~ Kasim age 22
(Interpreted to mean: I have a specific focus and things to accomplish,
if I stop, if I lose my focus I will die or go back to undesirable
conditions)

My trauma story starts around 1986. I was seven years old, in the second grade and one of five children. I was the middle child, two older and two younger siblings at the time. The late eighties was the onset of a historical trauma for many black families throughout the United States. It was the beginning of the *crack era.* Crack cocaine was a key factor in the continued destruction of our most sacred spaces as Afrikan people (our families and communities). Nineteen eighty-six was the birth year of my (multi-talented) sister. It was also the year my father became chemically dependent. My father was a handsome, articulate, athletic, charismatic and strong-willed man from the south (Cotton plant Arkansas). None of these great qualities would keep him from living out his trauma story and helping to create mine.

The backstory on my father and the context of his trauma that would eventually create mine is that he is the grandson of a doctor that he never met. He is the son of an African and native woman whose mother was from the tribes of Florida and whose father was a medical doctor (Dark skinned immigrant Muslim). A man my father and grandmother never knew. My father is also the son of a (Cuban and Panamanian) man that came from Jamaica. My father John Rudell Withers was named after his father, John Esther Withers. John Esther was described as a very intelligent, verbally, physically and emotionally abusive man with a strong personality, terrible drug addiction and womanizing behavior. John Ester was abandoned and found eating out the garbage with his brother Prentis before being put in an orphanage and eventually adopted.

My father spent his early years living in a *shotgun* house (where you can see from the front of the home to the back all on one level) with three older siblings and one younger. For eight years my father witnessed physical, verbal, emotional, and drug-induced traumatic events. I remember asking my father to tell me about the stairs in his house, and he replied, "What stairs?!" I asked him to tell me about the stove, and he said, "What stove?!" In humor and just, I would say, "Well, tell me about the roof," and he would say, "What roof?!" I would answer, "Come on daddy y'all didn't have a roof?!" He would say, "No, not like you think, not like this roof. The roof we had you could see through it, it didn't always keep rain or the weather out."

My father was the best storyteller, and he would keep my siblings and me entertained through the toughest of times telling us scary stories and fables from the south. He would also tell us stories of his childhood being hungry, his older brother hunting blackbirds with a single pellet BB gun that he would dig out of the birds and reuse. My father never laughed when he told these stories. My father John Rudell would also tell stories of his first experiences here in Minnesota, the discrimination he faced, the embarrassment of social services, the community his family became part of, and the people who influenced his mind.

A highlight in the backdrop of my father's life was his experience as a youth going to Jimmy Lee recreation center or Oxford as some know it. *Let's go big O!* That was the slogan my father would repeat with a smile on his face when he spoke of his experience there. John Rudell Withers was a member of *The Iron Five Men* (a youth team from Oxford that won a state championship in basketball with only five players where my father was the star point guard). My father John Withers was also a member of a youth team from Oxford that won a state championship in baseball where he was the star pitcher. He would remind us as children how he pitched a shutout, no hitter! And yes, of course, he was the star quarterback for Oxford's football team. My father dominated in sports and became most known for his basketball talent *John could step two feet past half court and hit bottom every time!* I heard this everywhere I went from older men that had a chance to watch my father play the game. I even heard it from members of the Mauer (uncle of Minnesota Twins star Joe Mauer) family as they referred my basketball games.

Central high school was where my father attended and graduated and where I would later attend, play basketball and graduate. My father was gifted physically and intellectually; he particularly enjoyed Math. As things would have it, my father moved out on his own at the age of 16 years old, met my mother (Marie Swan 17 years old) and began a family. In his junior year of high school, my father quit the basketball team during a game against a Minneapolis rival when he felt the coach wasn't playing him enough.

At the young age of sixteen, my father would leave behind his boyhood and immerse himself in the role and responsibilities of manhood. My father and mother had an apartment together, he worked, graduated high school, and went on to attend control data institute to learn trade skills. He deferred his dreams for his responsibilities and likely due to some fear and lack of support. My father and mother pressed forward together building a life together, and in August of 1979, I was born! Life was great in seventy-nine, my parents were in a building stage focused on forward progress. I watched them buy their first home, new cars, go to concerts, laugh, have family nights, engage the entire neighborhood, and have A-1 credit. This was life for my siblings and me until 1986 when we witnessed all of these wonderful life dynamics fade away. I would later learn that our losses and destroyed family health were the consequence of un-mastered appetites, lack of family resource and community support.

Responsibility & Accountability

We as Afrikan men have to raise our boys to be responsible and accountable. We have to inform them of their duties and context as men in training. We teach this through *parallel process* of first demonstrating responsibility and accountability ourselves. A boy needs to first see the model in action then informed of its function, intentionality, and end products. To be *responsible* means *to do What needs to be done, When it needs to be done and How it needs to be done.* Responsibility is therefore an acting or demonstrating characteristic. This character trait has to be proceeded by accountability. To be accountable is *to commit mentally and emotionally to a role and its duties while fully accepting the consequences of your actions.* Therefore, accountability is a cognitive and emotional characteristic. Accountability generates the psychological and spiritual context to carry out responsible actions/behavior. If we agree on these definitions, then we can also agree on the consequences of their actions, non-action, and/or partial actions. The effects are either positive psychological, emotional, and behavioral characteristics that help to transform boys to men or negative psychological, emotional, and behavioral characteristics that retard and prevent boy to man transformation. Again the results are either complete personhood or fragmentation. As black men, we have to be committed cognitively and emotionally to our (Black women) complements, our (Black children) legacies, and our (Black diaspora) communities. And we have to do whatever needs to be done to protect and secure their futures whenever the situation calls for it to be done and however the circumstances demand it to be done! Our healing is connected to living out these attributes and our sons' health and ability to remain strong and whole is connected to learning and applying these attributes. It is imperative that we understand and uphold these qualities in times of emotional and cognitive abundance as well as in circumstances of debilitated emotional and psychological capital. We are men well transformed beyond our maleness, capable of working through emotional dysregulation and cognitive distress. We have exercised the characteristics of responsibility and accountability into the essence of our beings and we will not withdraw from them and risk harm to ourselves, our children, partners or communities. This has to be our ardent commitment with unwavering resolve. That means if we chose to take actions that caused us to be fathers, we accept responsibility and accountability for that role without condition. It means to carry out and uphold the rights of black women to be loved, revered, protected, consulted, and prioritized with top priority irrespective to blood relation or sexual partnership. This is the creed of healed Afrikan men that must be fortified through our practices as we raise healthy strong Afrikan boys into men! These are essential tools of transformation for black boys and fragmented Afrikan men. These are tools to work on ourselves with meticulous, strategic, and fantastic rigor that we should be transformed into our best and complete potential.

The Afrikan man is comprised of finite and infinite energies. He possesses both physical and metaphysical attributes, and his success is contingent upon equilibrium and balance between the two. The physical attributes of Afrikan men (our bodies) serve as a reminder of our need for limits and boundaries while our metaphysical attribute (our souls) inform us of our limitless potential and desires.

The natural state of Afrikan men is to progress and mature into a divine balance between excess and deficiency. The Afrikan man has to learn to master self-discipline of his various appetites that have unending potential. The spirit can consume in excess; it has transcendent abilities to reach beyond physical limitation. And just as the physical body serves as a container for the spirit, so must the Afrikan man learn to contain and balance his desires in a manner conducive to his natural state.

How easy it is to spot the excess and deficiency of the Afrikan man's spirit as we manifest our acute and obtuse disproportionality through externalized behavior. As black men, we tend to follow both our biology and social conditioning. Our reproductive organs (penis and testes) operate with internalized followed by externalized processes. The penis is literally filled (internally) with blood in order to become erect to function or (externalize) the desire of the man. Additionally, the semen from the man travels (internally) from the testes of the man through the urethra to again externalize or release the internal workings of the self. This exact process although a natural function of man's biology is also used with (excess) perversion to socialize Afrikan men into unnatural states of being.

The Afrikan man has been removed from his right mind and convinced that he is less than human, unworthy, and above the universal law of complement (wholeness). In our (internal) detour from full personhood through the removal of our correct cultural understanding, we have become in totality acting out organs. We have internalized pain, therefore, we act out pain upon others. We have internalized objectification, therefore, we act out on our women, children, and community as if they are objects. We have internalized partial personhood, therefore, we act in our families with partial responsibility and partial accountability. We have internalized deficiency, therefore, we act out the rage of neglect through addiction and extreme indulgence in our desires. Brothers, we have been acted upon, we have internalized that behavior and we are acting out on those closest to us and most in need of us. Our behavior is a function of *arrested development*. We are stuck in a state of infantile and early adolescent development. We are demonstrating very little management of our appetites and no mastery of self-discipline. Therefore we act out and upon instead of acting for and with. Afrikan brothers, we have developed the psychology of our oppressors. As a result of not seeing ourselves as (subjects) complete people, we act upon our complements and legacy as (objects) incomplete people used as a means to an end. In order to heal and return to our natural state, we must work from the inside out identifying our imbalance and seeking its complement or restorative quality. If we have become rigid in our thinking and actions as a result of fragmentation, then we must explore and seek flexibility to bring balance to our lives. If we have become selfish as a result of neglect and unappreciation, then we must explore and practice empathy to restore our equilibrium. If we were allowed too much freedom and power, we must engage restraint and humility to make us whole. Our journey is difficult, but it is possible.

I recall as a teenager sitting in a room alone with my father asking him, "How did you get addicted to drugs?" His response was nothing short of divine wisdom from an old sage; he said, "Compromise, I compromised my values. It's like opening a door without full knowledge of what's behind it. It quickly overwhelms you without preparation." I could feel the power and meaning in my father's words without any further explanation. I have always recognized my father as a man of diligent preparation, high intellect, phenomenal will, outstanding creativity, and supreme confidence. Therefore, hearing him say compromise was a road to destruction and overwhelm, I invested my attention and resolve to carry this wisdom into action. However, it was carried out with imperfection and fallibility. I would have to undergo my own experience of compromise to learn a valued lesson of mastering self-discipline and controlling my appetites. I would later interpret my father's identification of compromise as a simplified understanding of mastering self-discipline and controlling our appetites. My father was speaking to his departure from his training and transformation, which involved learning to master self-discipline and control his appetites. His compromise was an exercise in looking for immediate satiation and resolve of his emotional desires. His compromise was in fact regression to infantile behavior, my bowels are full, so I relieve myself where I am, my penis is hard so I stick it anywhere it will fit to release its stimulation. Poor control of an emotional appetite and weak implementation in self-control resulted in non-discriminatory behavior with self-harming effects.

In my reflection on *self* and work with black men and black boys, I have begun to note the pattern of deficient responsibility and accountability as it pertains to our role within the family. Our emotional intelligence and endurance is severely lacking. And that deficiency has two significant consequences for Afrikan families: decreased capacity to communicate and interact at the (emotional language) frequency of Afrikan women; incongruent response and fortitude to the needs of Afrikan children. Therefore, black women are left isolated, un-engaged, misunderstood, over-utilized, and in unsatisfying partnerships; while black children are subjected to increased fatherless or partial encounters, reactive behavior, and unsatisfying emotional father engagement. These experiences are the results of fragmented personhood that offers partial emotional accountability and partial psychological and behavioral responsibility. Afrikan men, it is easy to spot this area of needed healing by the excuses we offer when confronted with that for which we are accountable and responsible.

I have heard it too many times, *"I'm not with my kids because Minnesota is a woman's state. They just gave her the kids and all the rights. I have to pay this high ass child support. My kids ain't seeing none of the money.* I recognize the injustice of our judicial system and the intentional strain it creates specifically to keep black families *broken* and divided, but brothas stop it! In many cases, it is our lack of accountability and responsibility that has us stop short and not commit all of our resource or energy to our proclaimed desired outcome. In fact, many times the outcome we are looking for is to evade or lessen financial, physical, and emotional responsibility on ourselves. Are we in courts arguing, *"Hey if the child gets sick in the middle of the night I need to be the one to take them to the emergency room. If the child is falling behind academically from the emotional distress of having their family ruined, I need to miss work and be at the school meeting with teachers and counselors.* No, I bet a judge has rarely heard this argument or position from a black man in court. Afrikan brothas this is not pathology nor criminalization of behavior, this is a reflection on *self* with the intended purpose of healing. Let us self-identify and embrace our excess and deficiency that we should gain mastery over our appetites and be restored to complete personhood. We deserve it, our families deserve it, our community deserves it, and the world deserves it. Healing is intrapersonal. *If there is no enemy within, the enemy outside can do us no harm!*

Success is in your routine

In my childhood as a black boy, my life was filled with ritual and routine. My house, my neighbor's house, my grandparents' home, and my community was full of expected routines and rituals to be followed. Every morning as a child, I would wake, come downstairs, and start with a request to my mother for something, *"Momma can I get some fruit? Can I go outside? Can I play in the basement?"* It didn't matter what the request was, my mother's response was always the same, *"Did you do your hygiene when you woke up? Get upstairs wash your face, brush your teeth, comb your hair, and straighten your room before you ask about anything.*" I mean this was day in and day out communication that took place without discrepancy. The conversation only changed from my mother asking me these things to me telling my mother I did these things before making a request. The routines didn't stop there. Our house had a routine for everything, *wash your hands before going in the refrigerator, take off your shoes when you come in the house, say your blessings before you eat, elbows off the table, wash your face and hands before you eat, say may I, did you hear me give you salaam, thank you, yes and please.* The list goes on and on. These were cultural expectations in my home that were taught as routine and ritualized by occasion. Afrikan children need routine because their success is in their routine.

As an Afrikan child, routine helped me to organize, prioritize, and create structure. And with years of diligent practice of routines, I developed mastery of particular spaces. Routine is the repetitive and consistent commitment to purposeful action to achieve a specific outcome. Routine has to be implemented with perfection, endurance, and willfulness. A strong routine can pull you out from under traumatic circumstances and conditions. I used routine to organize the chaos happening around me, to drown out the noise of distraction and to create sacred space through predictable healthy patterns.

I was around fifteen years old when I consciously and independently created a purposeful routine with a specific goal in mind. I wanted to play basketball in college; I wanted to get out of the state, that was my goal. I played sports my entire life, but I only enjoyed playing not the work or practice that went into becoming elite. The summer of my tenth-grade year, I started a routine. I woke every morning, prepared all my clothes in a gym bag knowing that I wouldn't be home until late. I would meet my friend at the bridge on St. Anthony. We would cross the bridge and get to the gym right as it opened. For hours every day, we would do drills. After drills, we would play one on one until we got tired. We would change clothes, go to a nearby Chinese restaurant if we had money and get some takeout, then head back to the gym by four o'clock. That was the time everyone came to the gym to hoop. I would stay and hoop (attack mode) until the gym closed. This was my routine the entire summer. If I hung out with friends, it had to be after or around my routine. My routine told me what time to wake up, what to do, when to eat, and when to sleep. My routine kept me focused and safe. I followed this summer routine for the next two years of high school, and aside from lots of fights, one shooting and a pistol pulled on my friend, I managed to stay clear of the circumstantial traps that I saw happening around me. I never worried about being a teenage father because I didn't have a girlfriend and I wasn't sexually active. I was exempt from going to jail because I wasn't on the corner selling drugs or breaking into people's homes. My stress outlet was embedded within my routine, and my routine was keeping me safe and on track. I added something new to my routine around sixteen years old.

I was born and raised in the faith of Islam. I knew and my community knew I was a Muslim. I was black and I was a Muslim. Although I was raised with this understanding, my father always told me *it's on you. You know who you are and you know what you're supposed to do. If you choose not to follow, it's on you, I did my job. I gave you a clear message.* Around sixteen years old, I chose to add more value to my routine. I became adamant and committed to a religious pillar (praying five times per day). I didn't adhere to the prescriptive times for prayer, but I committed to completing them every day. Soon my commitment became a structured timely routine. I prayed morning, noon, afternoon, evening, and night as prescribed. My routine had become so strong that again it would inform where I went, what I did, and what I avoided. I would stop in the middle of a streetball game to get my salat (prayer) done. At first, people would stop and say, *"Where did they go? Where did the brothers go?"* A reference often used toward my older brother and I because you were sure to see us together almost everywhere. We would go pray, come back and start hooping again like nothing happened. Eventually, friends, acquaintances, and rivals knew, *"Yeah, they finna go pray. They'll be right back."* I took my routine wherever I went, admiration and respect seemed to follow. My basketball and religious routine became schema for other areas of my life including school and academics.

I attended St. Paul Central high school, the school with the longest history and reputation for International Baccalaureate (IB) program in the state. This was a program of advanced courses for students who excelled academically and were tracked for college success. I was in IB classes from 9th to 12th grade. However, it wasn't until my junior year that I excelled in these classes. Without consciousness, the schema developed from my basketball, and religious routine was being generalized to school and academics. I received mostly A's and a few B's my junior and senior year of high school in advanced classes because of the routines I programmed into my mind and body. Years later, no children out of wedlock, no criminal background, no drug or alcohol addiction, several college degrees, married fifteen plus years, and a business owner. All of this coming from an environment of chaos, instability, and distress. If anyone should ever ask me how to become successful, I will tell them simply, *"Success is in your routine."*

The key to success for Afrikan men and boys is mastering our appetites. An appetite is simply our desires, our wants, and our cravings. The human appetite is insatiable, it has infinite potential, therefore, it becomes the work and training of Black boys to learn restraint and mastery of these desires. In order to develop mastery over our appetites, we must create *A routine of conscious discomfort*. Our routine of conscious discomfort has phases that propel us to a state of mastery. The first phase is *Critical Consciousness*. Critical consciousness is the process of self-examination as well as environmental examination (person in their environment). In this phase, we construct a unique plan that removes us from environmental stressors (that illicit personal desires) by engaging in self-work. The second phase is *Newness*.

Newness is aligning our psychological disposition with our behavioral experience. In newness we allow ourselves flexibility in thinking to make adjustments. We allow ourselves to be awkward, feel uneasy, feel unsure, and make mistakes. In the newness phase, we are gentle with ourselves by accepting non-mastery. The third phase is *Consistent persistence.* Consistent persistence is the process of repeating behavior over and over while re-aligning our psychology to seek mastery. This is the process of repetition accompanied with commitment to not giving up until the goal is obtained. The final phase is *Self-actualization.* Self-actualization is refined behavior and thinking that demonstrates mastery over our desires. This is the achievement of politically informed behavior (limiting setting or abstaining) for the purpose of (achieving a desired outcome) improved wellness.

PRINCIPLE 1 IN ACTION
Healing/Raising look like

- **Black boys doing chores around the house.**
- **Black boys participating in programs during the week that demand task completion.**
- **Black men paying for their children's activities, clothing, housing, and education.**
- **Black men being consistently physically and emotionally present with their children.**
- **Black men engaging Black women with consistent support and unwavering reverence.**
- **Black men and boys discriminating what they do and don't do based on the best interest of the family.**

- **Black men and boys establishing prayer, meditation, fasting, and exercise routines.**

PRINCIPLE II
Acting in before acting out

"I've had this feeling inside me since I was eleven years old and it has never gone away. I know I'm supposed to do something great that will benefit people." ~ Kasim age 19
(Interpreted to mean: Finding our best self is done by searching our innermost {selves} emotions and our greatness becomes help for other people).

Silence is golden

Growing up, I had the opportunity to spend valuable moments with my grandfather. He was a handsome man from rural Missouri of high-yellow complexion, ex-military, and a fourth-grade education. Among the many lessons I learned through our time together was the importance of silence! My grandfather (Shirley Swan) was a gamesman, hunting, fishing, you name it he could do it, and he was good at it. Late Spring and Summer was our time, fishing season! Grandpa loved to go fishing; I remember going with him a few times as a young boy (9 years old). However, it was in my adolescence that I would learn to appreciate the wisdom behind our fishing adventures.

Every Saturday or weekend opportunity, my grandfather would call me on the phone, *"Hello, is this my fishing buddy?" "Yes, grandpa." "Okay we are taking the boat out tomorrow. I'll be by in the morning, be ready." "Yes, grandpa."* I could hear the joy and excitement in my grandfather's voice. My grandfather was up in age by the time I was a teen, not too old to drive a car, hitch, and dock the boat, remember all the best fishing lakes or routes to get there, but old enough not to be able to distinguish me from my older brother. To grandpa, I was "his fishing buddy," and my brother was the "boxer!" My grandfather engaged us through his passions and his beliefs about our connectedness to his passions. My brother was a great fighter, winning lots of street altercations and because my grandfather loved boxing, he always invited my brother to watch boxing matches and encouraged him to become a boxer. I was quiet, observant, and didn't say much around adults, so my grandfather loved taking me fishing. Grandpa had three rules for fishing days, we talk on the drive, quiet on the boat, and catch as many fish as we can. My grandfather never told me he had three rules, he showed me. On the way up to the lake, my grandfather would talk, tell jokes, laugh, ask questions, and make pit-stops for snacks. But on the water, he was silent with an occasional word "got another one."

We always went fishing in the early morning (right before sunrise). On the drive to the lake, I would usually watch the sun come up over the horizon. We would hit the lake with our lunch, bait, bucket, and reels. The air off the lake was cold in the morning even in summer. Grandpa would get in the boat and give it some speed for the first few turns on the lake. The closer we got to our fishing spot on the lake, I would notice him drop the speed until the motor was barely revving. Grandpa would look and say, *"Put it down,"* and I knew that meant lower the anchor on my side. We would bait our hooks and cast out our lines. Grandpa was an experienced fisherman, he fished with an open-faced dropline; I was a novice, so I fished with a closed-face reel and bobber. Grandpa fished by touch, I fished by sight. Grandpa could feel the slightest movement on his line while I sat patiently eagle-eyeing my bobber waiting to see it drop under the water! I didn't know then, but I recognize now the healing qualities and practices being taught to me on that lake.

The lake was my grandfather's *sacred space*, his healing space, his quiet space to be alone removed from worldly distractions and in harmony with creation. Over time I learned to embrace these gifts as well. I was never afraid of the water even though at the time I couldn't swim. My grandfather taught me to respect the water, to move with the water and to adjust to its waves and current. The water taught me flexibility. The cold air that made my skin prickly in the early morning by noon would be a cool breeze gently moving sweat from my eyebrow. The climate taught me complement and balance. I would sit in silence on the boat, focused on a single objective, attentive yet relaxed, thoughtful yet present. My emotions were present but none competing for the spotlight, each feeling peacefully taking its turn to inform my actions. Determined would tell my eyes to focus on the bobber diligently, calm would tell my arms and hands to be steady, excitement would say pull back when the bobber disappeared, and pride would tell me to smile at my grandfather when I would drop the fish in the bucket. Those fishing experiences with my grandfather taught me that silence is golden! They taught me that silence was vital to creating internal harmony and the wisdom of *acting in before acting out.*

Learning & Embracing emotional energy

Why are black boys taught not to be emotional? And what does it mean to be emotional? Afrikan boys and men are socialized to deny a natural part of themselves as a means to develop masculinity. However, instead of this process developing healthy traits for manhood, it develops imbalance within our Afrikan boys and teaches them to lie to themselves. It teaches them to neglect themselves and detach from their **spiritual information center.** Emotions are a universal language and spiritual energy that connects people to people and informs our actions. As our black boys are taught to only embrace a limited range of emotions, they are by consequence learning to limit their actions (behavior responses) and ability to connect with others. The end product of this socialized grooming is later identified in *Principle III (Our women and girls)* where Afrikan women refer to their partners as *Narcissistic.* Our community keepers are accurately identifying the arrested emotional energy and deficient emotional IQ being masked as *masculinity* in our black boys and men. A lack of emotional understanding and neglect of emotional use breeds internal conflict, produces unempathetic interaction and incongruent thinking and behavior patterns. This concept is demonstrated in the familiar phrase *I didn't mean to hurt you!"* This exemplifies incongruence in thinking and behavior resultant from deficient emotional intelligence. Black boys and men are acting out anger, rage, and frustration because we have suppressed insecure, overwhelm, and embarrassed. Therefore, we are out of practice with the behaviors that coincide with these emotions. To respond to the emotion insecure is to allow vulnerability. To respond to the emotion overwhelm is to seek help. And to respond to the emotion embarrassment is to admit imperfection and sensitivity. These are missing attributes in the lives of black men and boys that denote incomplete personhood. In order to counteract this imbalance and raise healthy black boys, we have to teach them to embrace the totality of their emotions and the congruent actions that connect them to the rest of creation.

As black men, we have to be deliberate in teaching our black boys to identify and trust their emotions. Every emotion functions as an informational sensation offering us a unique and specific behavioral response. If we are unaware or do not trust our information center, we will *act out* with incorrect internal information; thus producing actions that are incongruent with our thoughts and feelings leaving us conflicted and unsatisfied. Furthermore, if we are limited in our range of affect and emotional intelligence, we block our ability to be empathic and connect to the emotional state of others. And what we are left with are self-centered emotional exchanges, unable to understand only able to be understood. This is an imbalance of the greatest magnitude that is destroying healthy Afrikan family and community relationships.

Zoom In

Emotions are internal stimuli helping us to navigate the world around us and connect with other people. I recall as an adult (professional) peers discussing *Energy*. They were talking about something they could feel not see. At first, I misunderstood what they meant. I have a gift for reading non-verbal communication as do many black children. However, non-verbal communication is observable I could see the body language and discern its meaning. This was not what my peers meant by energy. They were speaking of emotional vibration emanating from people. I had spent so much of my adolescence and young adulthood denying and masking my emotions that despite being a helping professional, I was stunted in my ability to identify or feel the *Energy* of others. In reflection, I believe my choice to work primarily with boys and men for the early part of my career aided in blocking my ability to feel *Energy*. In my late twenties, I intentionally began working more with girls. It was a space of newness. I had to find new ways to relate and develop different skills to connect. At times I felt awkward, unsure, and hesitant.

The birth of my daughter, as well as my work with girls, guided me into a space of personal reflection and self-development. I used both clinical and cultural skills to identify pattern, formulate suppositions, and reflect my findings inward. After a few years of learning from girls, being taught by my daughter, and self-reflecting, I was able to awaken some very dormant senses. The day I noticed the shift in my emotional intelligence and ability to sense (emotional) energy I was at work. I was going through my usual routine walking the building greeting familiar faces. I saw a colleague and said hello, she smiled and responded the same but as I walked past her, I literally felt a strong sensation go through my body. I had no idea what I was feeling, but it felt heavy. I kept walking, and went to my office for a few minutes to process. I was close to dismissing, denying or writing off the experience when I made the choice to trust my feelings. I went back to where I saw my colleague and sat down next to her (facing forward not making eye contact) and said, *"I'm not trying to be in your business and you don't have to say anything to me but I felt a heavy energy come off of you earlier. And I just want you to know my door is always open."* I walked away and never looked back. I felt a sense of relief even though my co-worker never affirmed anything was wrong. A few hours later, there was a knock at my door, my co-worker entered and closed the door. Now, this was non-verbal communication I was confident in. She sat and told me of a recent experience that was weighing heavy on her. I was humbled and joyed to have made that *Energy* connection.

This anecdote should not be misunderstood as mystical or me unlocking some mutant capability. No, I am simply illustrating the hopefulness and possibility of healing for black men and boys as we learn and embrace the full range of our emotions. I am offering the possibility of being able to connect emotionally to black women and girls in a manner that allows us to be of support by being in tune. Finally, I am speaking to untapped potential within black men and boys that affirms *being emotional* (having emotional intelligence) as part of masculinity.

Cleansing hate and accepting self

A core hurt for many black men and black boys is **acceptance**. In fact, it is a core hurt for black women and girls as well. This hurt is a byproduct of the social context that Afrikan people exist within all over the world. However, this is particularly so in the United States. Every institution within the United States is built upon outgrouping based on difference and *acceptance* based on conformity or assimilation. This is the case starting as early as five years old. A black child enters their first institutional experience (school) and is being examined and assessed for personal diversities that will either be accepted or rejected based on organizational values and social norms. They call this identifying if your child is *school ready*. However, the real identification is, will your child conform to the cultural-political constructs of *the system*? At five years old, an Afrikan child is undergoing operant conditioning that is teaching, reinforcing, and extinguishing values and beliefs about *self* in the institutional (school) environment. Operant conditioning *can be described as a process that attempts to modify behavior through the use of positive and negative reinforcement. An individual makes an association between a particular behavior and a consequence.* These values and beliefs will eventually be internalized as *self-love* or *self-hate*. Every thought, emotion, and action by a black child in this environment will be validated, rewarded, punished or invalidated based on its support or potential threat to (status quo or norms) of the institution.

This form of social conditioning shapes the **acting out** behavior of black boys and black men as they learn self-hate or self-acceptance. Afrikan boys and men need healthy family and community support systems to navigate these institutional spaces effectively. In fact healthy family and community lay the groundwork and political disposition for black boys and men to discern self-love (accepting self) from self-hate (rejection of self). Healthy black family and community systems teach Afrkan boys and remind Afrikan men of their history as to never be lost or misguided into self-hate.

The binary of self-hate and self-acceptance' can be behaviorally deceptive or misunderstood. Many black boys are taught by parents to try and fit into systems that are not made or accepting of them as full complete cultural beings. As they attempt to fit in, they become acquiescent to *hidden curriculum* and *hidden agendas.* This is not placing blame on black parents who are trying to ensure their child benefits from the social privileges of education. No, this is simply a call to Afrikan parents reminding us that our children have to be equipped with better tools and support while attempting to receive benefit from any institution that was not built with our interest in mind. The intricacy and embedded nature of these destructive psychological messages within many institutions can be difficult to identify. Therefore, it requires a framework for psychological, social, emotional, and behavioral assessment. As I have observed and experienced the details of this phenomena throughout my life and the lives of others, I took time to organize its pattern into a concept I refer to as *Typecast theory.* This theoretical explanation was formed by concepts introduced to me in the brilliant writings of Carbado and Gulati's book Acting White.

Typecast Theory

Typecast theory suggests that black boys and black men are organized into five categories by institutions,.which predict environmental responses. Each typecast is associated with either positive or negative (reinforcement) responses based on exerting or arresting political and racial energy. These five typecasts are the lens by which black boys and men learn self-hate or strive toward self-acceptance within institutions. Most traditional institutions have five categories to place black boys and men in to determine how it will act and interact with them. These categories are *The Angry black, The Good black, The Deviant black, The Entertaining black, and the Dangerous black.* These typecasts are placed upon Afrikan boys and men based on observable behavior and perceived cognition. These groupings are not discussed nor written down explicitly instead they are connected to the attitudes, beliefs, and values that construct the organization's social climate better known as the status quo. Here is a brief outline of each typecast.

The *Angry black* is seen as politically oriented and race-conscious but lacking resources and/or strategy to effectively carry out his consciousness of racial marginalization and social injustice. Additionally, the *angry black* may or may not possess the titles associated with having achieved a formal education.

The ***Good black*** is seen apolitical, upholds the status quo, race neutral, and can be used for monetary benefit. The *good black* may possess the titles associated with having a formal education as well as hold a rich, middle class or working class social identity.

The ***Deviant black*** is characterized as criminal-minded, breaks rules/laws, a social pariah or miscreant. The *deviant black* is often used as a label to discredit and neutralize the work and potential of the angry and dangerous black. This typecast is also used to justify incarcerating or killing the *dangerous or angry black*. A tangible example is media reports stating that Philando Castile was under the influence of marijuana when stopped and brutally murdered by a local police officer. Another example is Trayvon Martin cited as ditching or skipping school in association with his brutal murder by a lawless citizen.

The ***Entertaining black*** is seen as apolitical, upholds the status quo, race neutral, and able to be used for monetary benefit as well as distraction. The *entertaining black* may receive preferential treatment or find favor with ownership because of their talent that brings revenue to the organization such as athletes or any other politically neutral cash cow.

The ***Dangerous black*** is seen as politically oriented, race-conscious, challenges the status quo, possesses resources to carry out thoughts and declarations, strong ability to influence others, and keen intellect. The *dangerous black* is often educated formally or informally. These are your Malcolm Xs, Marcus Garvey, and Kwame Ture's.

Typecast theory is a conscious and subconscious (fear based) construct used to influence the thinking, emotion, and behavior of Afrikan boys and men. In fact, it is a social instrument used to differentiate threats from benefits easily. A black boy or man that has allowed themselves to become a benefit has typically done so in hopes to secure a social-monetary interest while compromising their humanity. Likewise, Afrikan men and boys positioning themselves as a threat have likely done so to their own social-monetary detriment while preserving their humanity. Typecast theory poses a treacherous and complicated decision matrix for black boys and men.

Black men and black boys *acting out* in ways that destroy our image, integrity, sense of wholeness, family and community systems is an act of socially conditioned self-hatred. The problem is that these are often black boys that fit the typecast of dangerous or angry black. Black boys that began the early part of their life excited about their blackness and willing to say so. They were race conscious and politically activated and as a result they were taught (self-hatred) they were *bad.* I am offering us the opportunity to act in, source causality and conditioning so that we can act out in our best interest. Acting in requires us to connect to our political self, our balanced self, and our cultural self. The self that puts *us* before *I*, the self that rejects individualistic and self-centered thinking. A black boy or black man can only be conditioned into self-rejection or self-hatred when we are concerned exclusively with our individual situation. Self-acceptance is understanding that *self* is always in reference to the collective black self. Our politics must always be governed by an internal force that embraces the cultural wisdom of *I am because We are.*

Zoom In

It is improbable that black boys and black men will go their entire lives without interacting or coming in contact with institutions that will solicit their conformity or offer opportunity to exchange cultural worldview and humanity for social status or finances. Therefore, it is with a debt of gratitude that I pay my respect to our institutional *critical care agents*. The people standing in the gaps for our black men and boys teaching us the skills and connecting us to resources that allow us to practice self-love. They are the *critical care agents* as described by Sonia Nieto. The people who discern the uniqueness of each person within their environment and offer the necessary tools to navigate the space with wholeness.

About six years ago, my family had the benefit of receiving community support by a *critical care agent* (Ms. Fallon). Ms. Fallon is a black woman that worked as a teacher in the local *Freedom School* here in Minnesota. This sista is beyond phenomenal and understands the needs of black children and the tools necessary to navigate the school system. Ms. Fallon was the teacher of my then soon to enter kindergarten son Isa. Isa like all of my children is a gifted and unique soul. He is also my first son. I think my wife understood the magnitude and impact the world could have on Isa way before I did. My wife studied and nurtured Isa every day of his life and knew his unique gifts, learning preference, and temperament. She placed him in outdoor learning childcare for two years before starting kindergarten. My wife understood he was a kinesthetic learner, a curious soul, and a free spirit with a huge heart. She is and has always been protective of these characteristics. We had several conversations about if we should send him to a traditional school like our daughter. My wife's main point of contention was summarized in a simple statement, *"I will not let them crush my child's spirit."* She knew that the unique diversities that made my son who he is would likely be responded to with negative reinforcement within the schools as he would be identified as the *dangerous black.*

The summer before entering kindergarten, we sent Isa to Freedom school; a space we trusted because we trusted the leadership. A talented brotha and longtime friend (Emmanuel Donaby). We trusted this brotha, the talent he recruited, and the space he created. And he did not disappoint. Isa was assigned to Ms. Fallon's classroom. Every day we sent greatness out our home, and everyday greatness returned from freedom school! The emotional wellbeing, psychological integrity, and cultural values taught at freedom school were aligned with those practiced in our home. The freedom school space exemplified healthy community. Family nights were well attended, parents were constantly in the space volunteering, interacting, and collaborating. One particular family engagement day we had the chance to have a more intimate conversation with Ms. Fallon regarding her critical care. Ms. Fallon discussed how she was attending to Isa's unique gifts and empowering him with a strategy to bring them into his new environment.

Ms. Fallon said to us, *"Oh my God! Isa is so talented and brilliant. His personality is amazing, he is a leader, and he loves to participate. I noticed that he enjoys using his body to express himself and information. This is one of his strengths. Isa and I have been working on preparing him to use his strength in his new environment."* Ms. Fallon gave us a look like we both know a black boy expressing himself through movement in a kindergarten classroom will be looked at as a behavior issue. It was just a look, but we all understood the look. Ms. Fallon continued, *"So Isa is working on using movement for self-expression with some limits. I told Isa he could use as much movement and be as creative as he needs to from the waist up! I told him that next year in kindergarten he will spend more time sitting than he is used to and teachers will expect that he stay seated when responding to questions."* We asked Ms. Fallon how the modification has been going. She gave us a huge smile and said, *"It has been going great! He loves being able to use his body, and I love seeing him engaged, so we have an understanding!"* Isa went to kindergarten that Fall with a life lesson and a healthy self-concept. Ms. Fallon offered him an alternative to the five typecasts. She offered him full personhood, self-acceptance, and politically informed behavior. Thank you, Ms. Fallon, you are a critical care agent and a manifestation of healthy community in action!

This year Isa is moving on to middle school after six successful academic elementary years. Isa has tested in the top percentile of the state in Math and beyond proficient in all other academic areas along with having acquired French as a second language! That is not to say his elementary experience went without challenges. Every year of elementary school was socially and emotionally pressing with the exception of second and fifth grade. Those two years he was blessed to have critical care agents and master educators (Mme Eichten and Mr. Mang). They attended to his academic wellbeing as well as ensured that he learned self-love. Our family was fortunate to have their care as part of Isa's school experience. These two educators just like Ms. Fallon are more than school staff to Isa they are his aunt's and uncle. My wife spent many days at the school and we both spent many afternoons there in meetings. We understood that our presence and support would be the only thing to prevent Isa from falling victim to the assimilationist typecasts of *good black or entertaining black.* Additionally, we refused to have his political assertiveness and racial conscious behavior reacted to as the *dangerous or angry black* typecast. My wife and I have worked hard to teach Isa to act in (self-love & self-acceptance) before acting out.

Fear of another Black Athlete

If you ask Black children from the inner city "What do you want to be when you grow up?" A common response is sure to be a singer, actor, rapper, dancer, basketball or football player! There is no secret that Black children living under stress, marginalization, and trauma see themselves escaping their circumstance by becoming entertainers. Who created this vision for black children and what implications does it have for the future of the black community?

I spoke with a young man not too long ago, an 8th-grade African American male that enjoys football. At 6'1 and approximately 260 lbs, this young man is easily visible in a group of his peers. This young man who is struggling academically asked me, "Do you think schools are better today than they were when you were a kid?" I responded, "No, I don't think they are better." He affirmed my statement by saying, "Me either, I think schools are worse. Teachers don't care about students. I wish I grew up in the 80s or 90s when people cared." The young man went on to say, "I see some serious issues at my school and I want to do something about it. I want to make it a place where students are treated fairly. I see that black kids are treated differently at my school, and I want to do something about it." After speaking with the young man a few more minutes, he informed me that if he could, he would stop coming to school and play football all day. He let me know that he loves football and has a dream to play in the NFL so that he can take care of his family. He said, "Yeah, I wish I could just work on my dream all day and not have to come to school." The encounter with this brilliant and politically charged young African American male had me asking the question, "What is the consequence of having another black athlete?"

In 2017, with overt racial oppression, discrimination, and killing of unarmed blacks throughout our nation by law enforcement, the community has been devastated, reactive and explosive in a manner similar to the 1960s. Yet, with this resurgence of black political activation to address racial injustice, the majority of black athletes have been quiet, brief, and reluctant, to use their voice or platform to discuss racial realities. Is it that black athletes don't care, are unaware, or are simply too scared to get involved?

I think Charles Barkley expressed most accurately one nuance of group conditioning that characterizes black athletes when he said, "I am not a role model!" Here it is a black man from the south, humble beginnings, saying I feel no responsibility to those coming behind me or those sharing my social reality. He is saying, I choose to detach from the shared experiences of others no matter what our common struggle, and I am here to look out for me! Additionally, I believe black athletes, for the most part, have become terrified and rendered courageless by the mere thought of losing fame, money, and the opportunity to play their childhood game (i.e., social, emotional, and financial castration).

In order to better understand the plight and psycho-social engineering of black athletes, you have to place them within the historical context of Afrikans in America. Historically, European psychology has used the methodology of "if you can name it, you can tame it" to study, pathologize, and dominate any group or organism that it has encountered. The Afrikan was and is no exception. Historically, white America has used five typecasts to organize and create methods of interacting with blacks. The *Angry black; the good black; the entertaining black; the dangerous black and the deviant black*. Two of these typecasts are amenable to the agenda of white America, two typecasts are direct threats to the mission of white supremacy and one typecast is used to attack the black community. We won't address all five of these typecasts. However, we will examine the typecast that characterizes the psychology and behavior of the black athlete.

The "entertaining" black is a politically neutral persona. They do not engage in behavior, conversation or thought that could possibly disturb the status quo. The entertaining black typically finds him or herself in alignment with white values and in servitude to white masters. They usually function as both a monetary benefit as well as entertaining distraction for white America. Entertaining blacks are likely to be elevated in status over other black typecast and held as a goal or position to aspire. This typecast usually finds itself in episodic encounters with value schizophrenia as a result of the psychological engineering of their newly constructed mind. The entertaining black walks in the agonizing crosshairs of success and subjugation.

The black athlete appears to neatly fit within the social construction of the typecast *entertaining black*. A painful and tormented space it must be for black athletes to be placed on a highly visible platform only to have their humanity and personhood reduced by arresting their executive functioning and silencing their political voice. The essence of manhood and womanhood is to exert executive functioning for the purpose of engaging in political action. Most children begin this process at age two. The **terrible twos** as they are sometimes referred denote a transitional time in development where children are beginning to assert their will and decision making by uttering the one-word phrase "No." At two years old, children let their caregiver know that they have recognized their human right to choose what they will and won't do based on personal interest/politics. How is it possible to take some of the most resilient, physically dominant, and action-oriented people in our population and completely pacify their natural instincts? The answer is simple, however, the process is sophisticated. I will articulate both the answer and the process used to construct and keep in check *the entertaining black.*

A person's life can be dissected into a few basic domain areas such as work, community, family, and school. Successful negotiation of these areas inform the overall wellness of a person. Conversely, debilitated wellness is often informed by impairment in one or more of the mentioned domains. In the case of black people, the domain areas have specific and special cultural connotation that impact wellness or dis-ease, success or impairment. For black people, the family and community domains are *sacred* from a historical and cultural context, particularly in America. Healthy living for blacks in America is predicated on having a healthy family and or community domains. It is an expectation for black people that friction or impairment occurs in the work or education domains as a predictable consequence of historical institutionalized racism. Dr. Amos Wilson calls this understanding one of the *seven psychological strengths of black people. A healthy skepticism of you know who.* Healthy black family and community domains are politically activated and serve as a means of protection. So how does it work for the black athlete?

The entertaining black or black athlete is a social construction of dis-ease or impairment in the family and or community domains attempting to negotiate their wellness through the work and or education domains. The black athlete experiencing a sense of racial injustice and overwhelm is offered and taught cultural values absent of political context as a means of resolving their dis-ease. Black athletes are often pulled from their families and communities and taught that their new family, their brothers, their sisters are those people on the field, court, etc., with them engaged in struggle. These athletes are reminded of their cultural value and method of healing which is to work collectively with family and community to achieve a common goal. Black athlete, Ray Lewis, described this best when he said, "I've never known a brotherhood except the University of Miami and I still know no other brotherhood except the U." This social conditioning and psychological restructuring are enough to create a Michael Jordan, Barry Bonds, Allyson Felix, and many others. The black athlete has their cultural value (family & community) used to elevate the status of their organizations and owners. The political energy once used to restore justice to family and community is now used as a driving force to entertain. And as these black athletes recalibrate their values and energies with a purpose of self-preservation, self-upliftment, and self-appeasement, they become politically neutral to the obvious racial realities of their former families and communities. The black athlete through time and struggle develops a higher loyalty to that which they have built/invested (their careers) than that from which they have come. This becomes the dominant and pervasive manner by which black athletes choose to negotiate their new "politically correct" or politically neutral existence. The black athlete that adheres to the social order of *the entertaining black* can expect to carry on with little disruption of their conformed lives. However, if they choose to exert full personhood by thinking and acting as a politically charged human, they are met with the most fantastic resistance.

Today's example of a black athlete that has decided to resist the typecast of *the entertaining black* is Colin Kapernick. A highly favored and talented black professional quarterback who refused to subjugate his personhood and spoke out against injustice. The result, removal from his station, status, and ostracized by all organizations and ownership. To be direct, he was made an example of and is experiencing the psychological freedom afforded him as a human birthright. Like many others before him, Muhammad Ali, Mahmoud Abdul-Rauf, Jim Brown, Harry Belafonte, Fela Kuti, and many more Colin Kapernick has chosen full humanity to the 3/5th compromise of the black athlete or entertaining black! I respond to the question "What is the consequence of another black athlete?" Another black athlete that accepts the typecast and social construction of entertaining black means to accept a reduced humanity and live a fragmented existence unbefitting of their humanity. More importantly, it means to perpetuate an unjust social order and be used in the fashion similar to any other tool required for labor and financial gain. Let the statistics speak, (how many black athletes end up broke after their careers?). Black athletes AWAKEN and honor your complete personhood. Let not your talents, bodies, values, thoughts, and beliefs be bought and sold like modern-day chattel on the auction blocks of tennis courts, football fields, basketball courts, track fields or any other space of talent that we occupy. Be phenomenal, be complete, be human, be Beautiful Black Powerful People!

PRINCIPLE 2 IN ACTION
Healing/Raising look like

- **Black boys learning and expressing their emotions to other black boys and girls**
- **Black men asking black boys how they feel**
- **Black boys learning knowledge of their history**
- **Black men teaching black boys the importance of their history**
- **Black boys consistently being supported by their families in institutional spaces**
- **Black men consistently advocating on behalf of their black boys**
- **Black boys learning to be politically engaged and race conscious**

PRINCIPLE III
Reconciling cycles of hurt

"You were born with some "gifts," and although these gifts were given to you, you have to decide if you can move the needle or end the story in your lifetime. If not, know that you will pass them forward." ~ Kasim age 38
(Interpreted to mean: Some of our life challenges were things passed on from our parents and grandparents. If they were unable to be resolved in their lifetime, it's up to us to continue working to end the cycle or risk leaving the burden to our children).

It is of the utmost importance that Afrikan men raise Afrikan boys with discernment between *pain* and *hurt*. Our black boys have to become acquainted with pain, learn their pain threshold and build resilience by working through pain. Pain can be overcome with powerful psychological motivation, and it should be understood as an integral benchmark on the road to manhood and greatness. Pain is temporary, and it can be used to build human capacity and wellness. Hurt is not pain although it sometimes feels the same. Hurt can be caused by self or others; it happens to us. Hurt is destructive, debilitating, and maladaptive. Hurt does not build the human in capacity nor wellness. Hurt creates negative *programs* in the psycho-social-emotional operating system of black life. These programs are internal schema developed over time and experience that become cycles of hurt. In order to become healthy Afrikan men and raise healthy Afrikan boys, we have to reconcile these cycles of hurt by destroying these programs and adopting new health producing schema that becomes our automated responses to life's stresses.

The distress and cycles of hurt experienced by black men and black boys have without question reached *clinically significant* status. Our cycles of hurt have rendered us ineffective in particular areas of life denoting clinical significance. Clinically significant is *impairment in an individual's social interactions, capacity to work, or other areas such as family, school, and community that disrupt successful functioning.* For us as Afrikan men, impaired functioning in family and community tend to be both the source of our cycles of hurt as well as where we cause hurt. Family and community have caused us pain in our boyhood, and in return, we hurt our families and communities in assumed manhood. Therefore, it is our responsibility and commitment through healing that as we restore ourselves, we also restore and reconcile the cycles of hurt we have continued in our family and community.

The first step in reconciling our cycles of hurt is to identify the hurt and its historic origins. Better said by a cultural old wisdom, *"The village that hides the truth cannot expect to heal but pass on the pain."* Our cycles of hurt act as powerful programs stuck in our subconscious, felt in our hearts, and acted out with our bodies. A negative program and cycle of hurt that has followed me into my adulthood is verbal abuse. I have the ability to use my words to cut like a knife injuring those that I love most. This is a cycle of hurt passed down from my father and likely his father. I use to think it was a skill or a talent. Growing up I had the ability to see someone's vulnerable area, their weakness, insecurity, and fears. At twelve years old I was probably

71

better at psychoanalysis than most Freudian trained therapist. What I imagined to be a gift, something I could use to defend myself became a tool of malice to hurt others. If I became angry with someone, I would verbally assault their personhood. If I was hurting and wanted others to feel my hurt I would unleash my words and make people miserable. I thought I enjoyed causing hurt to others because of the pseudo relief and sense of power it presented. Only later in adulthood was I able to equate this false sense of gratification with my acquired taste and familiarity with dis-ease. Causing hurt through verbal abuse had become a familiar *program* to me and so I automated its response to my psychological and emotional sensations. I had learned how to hurt but not how to heal. More importantly, I had learned how to hurt *self*, meaning I attacked and took out my rage on those closest to me (family and community). This family *program* of verbal abuse is also a politically and socially constructed *program* imposed on the vast majority of Black psyche. Afrikan people have been taught to *roast, flame, get on, or* simply verbally disrespect one another as a form of entertainment, which is in fact a subconscious practice of self-hatred and rejection of self. This seriously debilitating *program* and cycle of hurt is called *Mentacide.* Dr. Bobby Wright has brilliantly identified, defined, and interpreted mentacide as the deliberate and systematic destruction of black minds. We have African boys and Afrikan men acting out their psychological dis-ease through negatively constructed programs. Our cycles of hurt can be verbal, physical, sexual, emotional, and other behavioral manifestations. No matter the form the hurt takes, it causes destruction and the likely targets are those we know best - family and community.

Zoom In

I recall as a young boy my mother and father sitting my siblings and me down to tell us that my father was on drugs. The conversation was extremely open and transparent, however, the content was definitely beyond my eight-year-old context. My parents' words were very simple, *"Kids we brought you all together to tell you something. Daddy is sick; he needs help, daddy is on drugs."* The look of shock and confusion settled on the faces of us as children. I remember a response by one of us, *"Why is daddy sick from being on drugs? We drink drugs all the time and don't get sick."* As kids, we use to call food residue in our water cups *drugs*. I think we heard our parents refer to them once as dregs and we misunderstood it as *drugs*. That was our point of reference for drugs at that age. We would later have a more clear understanding and point of reference for (street) drugs. I thank my parents for having the courage to name our family cycle of hurt and to present the information early.

In later years, I was reminded and exposed to the conversation about drugs and its relationship to my family. I grew up with the cultural practice that children don't sit around adult conversation. As a young teen, I remember visiting my grandmother (Mo'dear). I'm not sure if she was talking directly to me or if she was talking out loud and I was able to overhear her words, but that day she revealed the historical origins of drugs and the cycles of hurt it has caused within our family. My grandmother's children are divided between three different men (A Native man, an Island man, and African American man). Mo'dear is the matriarch of our family and a psychologist in her own right. She constantly analyzed behavior, causality, and interpreted for meaning. That day in my early teens that I visited Mo'dear, she revealed information that had a powerful impact on my life's decisions. She said, *"If you are a Withers, you better never do drugs because you have that island blood in you and once you taste it you become addicted."* She continued, *"And if you are a Binns or Simon, you better stay away from alcohol because you have that native blood in you and you will become an alcoholic."* Those words were lifelines for me and had particular value as I was old enough to testify to their truth. I was old enough, aware enough and honest enough to confirm these patterns of addiction within members of my family exactly as my grandmother had named them. I was a Withers, a descendant of Island ancestry from my paternal grandfather. He was a drug addicted man of Cuban and Panamanian descent. I believed my grandmother's words and decided at that moment to never use drugs as I had witnessed the destructive impacts on my household. I was not a Binns or Simon, however, I took the wisdom from my grandmother's words and reflected on my maternal ancestry. I recognized the potential threat of alcohol addiction that lay within the bloodline of my maternal grandmother (Nikkomis White-cloud) a woman of native ancestry. Again as a result of naming the pain and cycle of hurt I was offered the opportunity to reconcile and bring an end to my family cycle of drug and alcohol addiction through abstinence. Ending a family cycle of hurt is typically more difficult than hearing words and choosing not to engage in the behavior. My choice and ability to abstain from drugs and alcohol and reconcile a cycle of hurt was actually the culminating moment of at least two lifetimes of effort.

Reconciling cycles of hurt is about restoration and bringing balance back to our lives. This means we have to work in the present to reconcile our past in order to create alignment with our future. The work we do in the present is our healing. Drug use, abuse, and addiction is a stress response. However, when your stress response removes resources, prevents you from being present, inhibits your ability to attend to your responsibilities and causes you to be unaccountable, then it causes hurt. My father, a man that I loved and admired used drugs as a stress response and it caused hurt to my entire family. It caused so much hurt that my love and admiration became overshadowed at times by contempt, disdain, and disgust. My father's (addiction) response to stress was destroying the bond between son and father. It was pulling away and tearing down a system of protection. Over time I began to dehumanize my father, lack empathy for him, and pathologize his behavior as lacking effort or fortitude. I found it difficult to respect him as a man.

One night with just my father and me at home, we had a conversation that brought me to a new way of thinking. More importantly, we found a new way to *be* with one another. We found behavior that even in dis-ease could offer us the opportunity to heal. My father made a promise to me that night, a promise that he never broke. He told me, *"Kasim, I don't make promises because I know with my addiction I won't keep them but I'm promising you tonight that I will never put you in that situation again."* He continued, *"I need you to do something for me. You know what kills me inside? When I come in from being high, the look you give me. You don't look like I let you down, you look like I just gave up. You look like I've stopped trying. Kasim I try every day. If you can do anything for me, just don't look at me like I've given up because I haven't.* My father kept his promise, and I kept mine. I never looked at him like he gave up and in my heart, I believed he was trying. My father passed away in our living room almost two years after that conversation never having conquered his drug addiction.

Reconciling cycles of hurt calls for us to study and source the origins of the cycle. My grandfather (my dad's father) was addicted to drugs. I'm not sure about my great-grandfather, but it's possible he was too. My father grew up in a home where he witnessed his father's daily drug use as a response to life's stress. Reconciling cycles of hurt is not a single action or decision. Reconciling is more like *uninstalling* a program from a computer or phone; it takes time, work, and consistent action. The humanity restored to my father came to me in understanding and reinterpreting his actions. *I AM because WE ARE!* My dad saw his father use drugs daily. My father was what I use to hear people refer to as a *binge user.* That means he would use for days or even a week but would then be sober for weeks or months. As a child, discernment or appreciation of using every day versus *binge using* never crossed my mind. Later in life as I began to understand reconciling cycles of hurt as a process of *uninstalling* intergenerational programs, I was able to restore my father's humanity. My father (John Withers) was doing the hard work of *uninstalling* an intergenerational (unhealthy stress response) called drug addiction. When my father said, *"Don't look at me like I've given up because I haven't,"* I didn't know he was fighting not only for himself but all his children. My father's *binge use* of drugs was him fighting to *uninstall* drug addiction from the lives of his children. His time ran out before the uninstall completely took place, but when *I plugged back in*, I was able to finish what he started. I feel blessed and empowered to know that my father's fight was my fight and that we beat drug addiction together! Drug addiction is a common stress response and cause of hurt for many Afrikan families that tears apart family relationships. Although chemical and substance abuse is a significant cycle of hurt for black families it is not the only cycle.

Our women and girls

A cycle of hurt that demands immediate attention and reconciliation is the ongoing hurt caused to Afrikan women and girls by Afrikan men and boys. This is a paramount cycle of hurt that has been ingrained in the psychological framework of black men and boys through intricate and persistent social reconstruction. In my study of self and work with the Afrikan community, I have recognized this pattern and cycle of hurt as a pervasive dynamic.

In just the past year or so, I have witnessed a pattern of shared language amongst Afrikan women related to their "diagnosis" of their (black male) partners. I don't know if all of these black women collectively read the same article (very possible) or simply shared it on social media until it was read by every black woman I met this year. Whatever the case, these Afrikan women were telling me they believe their partner (a black man) has *Narcissistic personality disorder*. Hey, I'm not excluded from this group of black men. It was maybe two or three years ago the first time my wife referred to me as a narcissist. Yeah, two or three years ago, I know my wife likes to be ahead of the curve. Now do I (as a diagnosing psychotherapist) believe that all of these men including myself meet the criteria for *Narcissistic Personality Disorder*, absolutely not! So what does this shared experience and interpretation by Afrikan women mean for the psychological and behavioral health of Afrikan men? It is my belief and discernment that black women are speaking to a serious and real imbalance within the psychological framework and behavior of many black men.

In order to understand this imbalance that has produced a cycle of hurt, we have to identify the behavior and psychological disposition, source its origins and contrast it with healthy Afrikan (culture) worldview. Some of the characteristics of the narcissist is requiring excessive admiration, interpersonally exploitative, lacks empathy, arrogant, and obsessed with power. In relationships with Afrikan women, this can show up as underappreciating and not valuing the black woman's contribution. It may present as black men needing and demanding constant affirmation or positive feedback. It could be black men dominating the conversation (listen, don't interrupt, and it's over when I'm done) only willing to talk never to listen. It may also be identified as being dismissive or judgmental of the black woman's perspective and trying to solve her problems instead of supporting her in achieving her goals. Additionally, you may spot it in rigid, controlling encounters with finances, decision making, problem-solving, and future planning. Finally, the narcissistic behavior may look like need-based and driven interactions with the black woman (I'm in your face or being nice to you because I need or want something). A relationship with these forms of interaction and relational dynamics are definitely unhealthy and out of balance. So where did this thinking and behavior originate? We might make an easy assessment and say that it is a learned behavior from the fathers and grandfathers of these black men taught during childhood. Let us take an alternative route in sourcing this dis-ease.

A common practice that I use when searching for a solution to a problem is something called a *Zoom Out*. A zoom out is an inductive process of using the detailed behavior (the problem) and putting it into a container (the concept). The concept allows us to see the big picture. So take all of the imbalanced behavior that we just used to describe the *narcissist*. What is the (zoom out) concept? I offer as the concept or container *disrespect of the black woman*. Now that we have a container or concept, let's attempt to source its origins from the vantage point or concept of *disrespect*. And for this, I offer cultural worldview in the form of agreed upon and shared anecdote.

I'm thirty-eight years old, and in my lifetime there was an agreed upon and shared cultural experience related to the disrespect of black women. I'll get us there by asking a question to black people. If you are around my age or older, what is the one topic sure to cause a black boy to fight without hesitation? Hahaha yes, that's right disrespecting his (black) mother? Growing up you could talk bad about everything going on in a black boy's life, but if you mentioned his momma, you had to fight! This behavior affirmed the psychological and emotional disposition and connection that black boys had for their mothers. Black boys revered, protected the honor, cherished and loved their black mothers. This was their cultural worldview of the black woman. The black boy was trained to protect against *disrespect* to the black woman. So what happened and where did they learn to exchange this healthy orientation for the imbalanced and unhealthy psychology of the *narcissist?* Well, I like the observation made by rapper Lecrae as he characterizes assimilated thinking and behavior of black men with these words, *"They must be whores because the master rapes them and leaves the child. So dead beat daddy was taught to me way before my time.* The ugly truth about the imbalanced (disrespect) behavior toward black women and girls by black men and boys is that it is a construct of white supremacy. The psychological disposition of Afrikan men to disrespect Afrikan women is not culturally affirming. Therefore, it can only be a reconstructed psychological framework steeped in cultural deprivation and departure understood as dis-ease.

Afrikan brothers, the cycle of hurting our (Afrikan women) complements has to be reconciled and healed. If we understand that an assimilated mindset shifted our emotion and behavior into becoming disrespectful *Me Monsters,* then we have to conclude that reconciliation and healing are connected to the intentional behavior of *We. We* behavior is political, it recontextualizes experience and goals. Action is intentionally carried out with the purpose of a collective goal with communal values. That is to say, the sum total is greater than individual value, which dictates reverence, appreciation, and respect for the black woman, self, and what you are able to create together. As I stated earlier, I am not immune to this particular cycle of hurt. Therefore, I will offer information related to identifying the dis-ease as well as healing.

Afrikan men, I have worked with our community for many years and I have come to understand a dialectical dynamic within our (dis-eased state) of community. The dynamic adheres to words I've heard my father say many times throughout my childhood, *"The same thing that makes you happy can make you sad."* That is to say, love and hurt can be caused by the same source. Therefore, I know it is possible to hurt the people we love. To truly love is to be conscious of the conditions that create love and protect them to prevent causing hurt. The secret to reconciling the cycle of disrespect to our black women is attached to the conditions of their love. Two essential components of loving Afrikan women are *liking* them and being *nice* to them. If I'm lying, ask a black woman. Even better, the next time you are with an Afrikan Queen, and she says to you pleading, *"Just be nice to me. You don't even act like you like me,"* know you are two weeks away from having her explode on you in a fit of neglected rage! To be *nice* to our black women is the practice of showing empathy, patience, and emotional connectedness. To *like* our black women is to collaborate, show attention, reverence, and unwavering loyalty. These are the practices of black men and boys who seek to reconcile the cycle of hurt caused to our black women and girls. I stand firm and convicted on my decree, *"There is no healing of the black man without healing the black woman!"*

Cultural Domain Theory

Throughout my time serving the Afrikan community and working with us through our dis-ease and pain, I have come to see a pattern in our experience. Over time I have interpreted and organized these experiences (as a diagnosing mental health professional) into a pedagogical and theoretical framework that I refer to as *cultural domain theory*. This framework allows micro, mezzo, and macro-level insight into the breadth and depth of potential cycles of hurt experienced by black people as well as a strategy for therapeutic intervention.

As a psychotherapist, I typically deal with the life challenges of people when they have become *clinically significant*. Clinically significant refers to the impact of mental health symptoms within a person's life that has created impairment in at least one domain area. Basic life domains can be organized into *school, work, family, and community.* A client coming to seek therapy usually does so after experiencing a disruption in one of these domains. Therefore, an essential component of therapy is a reduction of mental health symptoms to produce effective functioning in the disrupted domain area. In my work with various ethnic populations, I have had the opportunity to contrast the Afrikan experience and navigation of life domains to that of white counterparts.

Cultural domain theory offers insight into the unique experience of Afrikan people and healthy psycho-social-emotional navigation of life domains. Black people participate in each domain area same as all other people. However, each domain should not be understood the same for Afrikan people because they are not experienced the same. As such, clinically significant must also take on alternative meaning for people of Afrikan descent. An Afrikan person experiencing (stress) impairment in the school or work domains should not automatically interpret this as illness. In fact, (stress) impairment in work or school domains may actually be evidence of healthy psycho-social formation. The foundation (of racism) that every (post-colonial) institution in America was built upon including work and educational institutions serve as debilitating *conformance* spaces for Afrikan people. Therefore, black people experiencing stress or impairment in these domains can be with full knowledge that their stress is partially the result of the political struggle to experience complete personhood within a toxic space. To be overwhelmed by the stress of these spaces is due to lack of sufficient support from family and community domains. Healthy family and community domains serve as protectants and success navigators for work and school domains.

Although many black people understand this truth, we often underemphasize its impact as we find the work and school domains necessary for survival and upward mobility. As we (black people) overlook the negative effects that work and school domains have on us as cultural beings, we overexpose and neglect to protect ourselves thus encountering real illness. And because our families and communities have already been wounded, work and school domains become daily experiences that help to debilitate or continue to weaken family and community domains.

Cultural domain theory repositions the psychology of Afrikan people to understand life domains as either debilitating or replenishing with attention and protection of those that offer wellness.

In my study of *self*, I have concluded that wellness creating domains are family and community. To be more specific, *healthy family and healthy community* are the only wellness creating domains. Healthy family and healthy community reduce stress and impairment in work and education domains for Afrikan people. Conversely, work and education can pose a threat to family and community functioning for blacks. Afrikan people instinctively know that healthy family and healthy community are wellness producing spaces. An anecdote that helped to validate and build (using grounded theory approach) one of the components of cultural domain theory was observed in Minnesota's public school system.

As I served as a school social worker in the public schools, I observed a fascinating cultural creation. Black children feeling the stress and overwhelm of their educational institution began to re-create relationship and space to protect themselves. I observed Afrikan students seek out Afrikan staff within their buildings and demand a reconstruction of their relationship. These Black students would refer to these Black staff as their *school mom, school dad, school uncle, school aunt, and so on.* These Black children were demanding their rights of kinship from Black adults to be protected, loved, and nurtured in a space that causes them distress.

Cultural domain theory insists that healthy family and healthy community are the wellness producing domains for Afrikan people and vital to our healing and thriving. Within this theory, we understand that healthy family and healthy community originate from emotional connectedness (spiritual protection), resides within our psychology (belief of accountability and responsibility), and is demonstrated behaviorally (through our politically driven actions). Additionally, cultural domain theory acknowledges the historical, persistent, political, and intentional actions by colonizers to debilitate and destroy healthy Afrikan family and community systems through the process of *cultural departure*. Cultural departure is a four-step/stage process (de-centering, psychological assimilation, behavioral activation, and legacy sickness) used to deconstruct and control the Afrikan mind. Therefore, understanding and responsiveness to impaired domain areas for black people dictate specific and intentional actions that address their causality.

Cultural Domain Theory conceptualizes work and education domains as training grounds for Afrikan people where distress denotes affirmation of political (complete personhood) struggle, not illness. Institutional data that verifies racial stratification and racial disparities validate the sickness offered to Black people in these spaces. Therefore, cultural domain theory emphasizes our strategic healing practice of family and community reconstruction within these spaces as supportive navigation methods to counter racially stratified data and disparities. Successful navigation of education and work domains for Afrikan people demand healthy family and community support, which is the only solution to address institutional racism. That is to say a commitment to protection, a practice of communal engagement, a spirit of togetherness, and emotional acceptance of Afrikan people by Afrikan people.

A practitioner or service provider implementing cultural domain theory must first assess functioning in each domain. If the Afrikan person or family has a healthy community and family functioning, then the focus of therapeutic support becomes psycho-education, skill building, and politicizing to create family and community support within the distressing (education, work, etc.) domains. However, if family and community are the impaired area(s) or cause of distress, then the practitioner sources the historical context of the impairment and creates space for the family and or community system to heal. Although family and community are understood to be the wellness producing domains for black people, it is with overwhelming data that hurt, harm, and dis-ease are often reported as originating or caused by family or community for Afrikan people.

Over ninety-five percent of the Afrikan people that I have worked with for almost two decades have reported family and community as the cause of their distress or reason for seeking help. Cultural domain theory addresses this information with the pedagogical approach that black healing has to be initiated by offering healthy family and healthy community experience through black-owned and operated services. That is to say, the psychological, social-emotional, and physical distress experienced by Afrikan people from their family and/or community as a primary concern has to be immediately engaged by demonstrating and offering healthy family and community experiences to counter their lived trauma. These therapeutic and professional experiences prep the psychological foundation to explore and resolve current, historical, and intergenerational patterns of family and community betrayal. The main construct in creating healing for Afrikan people is self-determination as this has been the calling card of constructed dis-ease in our community. Again cultural domain theory suggests that resolving impairment through a recreation of healthy family and community are mandatory for complete Afrikan personhood and true wellness. To reiterate, lack of self-determination and self-help are at the core of Afrikan dis-ease and has to be resolved through reflective and experiential self-help and self-determination experiences.

Cultural domain theory operates with the belief that hurt, harm, and dis-ease occurring to black people is a consequence of strategically dismantled family and community domains. We understand this as conceptual causality and therefore must be addressed as such. For example, divorce in the black community should be understood broadly as a function of lack of support and health in family and/or community domains. And the lack of support is a consequence of ongoing strategic dismantling of healthy Afrikan families and communities. Therefore, the specifics of any black divorce such as infidelity, abuse, etc., are all incidental contributors to the causal culprit which is organized dismantling of family and community support. That is to say, challenges happening within a black family are expected, however, to be overwhelmed by these conditions are consequences of strategically destroyed black family and community domains. Where are the black fathers and grandfathers that have time and wisdom to intervene when stress invades the home of black men? How available are black mothers and grandmothers to offer caregiving, wisdom, and nurturing when misbehavior peeks its head in the door of a black woman's home? Where are the neighbors, where are the counseling centers, churches, and mosques to hold the family system strong until they are clear of life's challenges? Again prevention and healing of clinically significant challenges for Afrikan people rest in the power of having and maintaining healthy family and community domains. Cultural domain theory acknowledges the phenomena of broken or fragmented Afrikan family and community support with clarity and truth that they are functions of oppressive political agenda being strategically carried out. As a result, cultural domain theory insists on the political action of reconstruction and (intrapersonal) healing of Afrikan families and communities by means of reconciling historical cycles of hurt.

Zoom In

I recall a time in my life feeling so distant from myself, from my essence, and from my natural state. I needed so desperately to find center as I witnessed myself in such a state of imbalance. I had no idea where to start. I felt a sense of despair and was unsure where to start looking for "me." I sat still and found "me" in the last place I left myself (inside my oldest son Isa Uthman).

My son Isa is an extraordinary young man, and when he was five years old without his knowledge, he helped transform my life. It was late one night in our home, and everyone (kids) should have been in bed. I saw my son walking the halls going from the back to the front of the house checking and locking doors. After his perimeter check, he came and kissed his mother, complimented her, watched her face light up with joy, then looked at me with a smirk and raised his eyebrows twice. I laughed and smiled back at my wife and said, "That's your son." Isa is such a kind and loving spirit. His actions that day triggered a memory of my childhood self, my essence, my natural state. As a child, I used to check all the doors in the house and kiss my mother the same way every night before going to bed. At that moment, I knew I could always find "me," the best of me, the natural me in the hearts and actions of my children. I also recognized the interconnected relationship being transmitted from father to son and son to father. I understood that keeping my son as close to his natural essence and spiritual disposition would take me returning to my own. My son needed me and still needs me to be healthy and healed so that he can remain healthy and whole. I will forever love my son for sharing that gift with me and reminding me of who I am. He did something for me when I was unable and unsure of what to do for myself. His spirit connected to mine and his grandfather's in that moment to reconcile a hurt that he never knew existed.

When I was a teenager, I remember my father being in despair and asking the question, "Why can I help so many people but nobody can help me?" This was while he and I were having a conversation and he followed that rhetorical question by saying, "Kasim, I'm not talking about you. You're a kid, I'm talking about these adults." Seeing my father in such pain and despair, I felt hurt that I was unable to help him. Well, my Isa 17 years later let me know just how I was helpful. Isa helped to reconcile a cycle of hurt in our family. He was being his best and unique self. He was demonstrating his contribution and commitment to *healthy family*. Every Afrikan boy and every Afrikan man has to identify and demonstrate daily their contribution and commitment to living as a *healthy family*.

Gifts given to me

A difficult lesson to learn that released me from the pain of guilt and shame was that I was given *gifts* as a child. I call them *gifts* not because they were offered to me as things to cherish but because they were things I wasn't born with nor did I ask for. These *gifts* are the unresolved traumas, imbalances, excess and deficiencies passed forward from my parents, grandparents, and great-grandparents. They were the things my parents likely hoped to protect me from yet became part of their unintended parenting.

Gifts often show up in our lives as hidden areas or blind-spots due to their common practice and accepted normality within our family, community or social context. And even when they are recognized as unhealthy practices of family members or even ourselves, we can minimize their impact or neglect to source their origins and the destructive consequences on our family system. In order to heal from our *gifts*, it is necessary to identify their origins, severity, family impact, and progress toward resolution and restoration. We are all carrying *gifts* whether we choose to acknowledge them or not. It is only a matter of stress that will bring these unhealthy *gifts* out. What I am referring to is that our *gifts* established by parents, grandparents or great-grandparents were unhealthy choices they made to cope with overwhelming amounts of stress. Therefore, these gifts if unresolved will, without doubt, reveal themselves in our lives under the correct amount of stress and because of our predisposition and non-restoration we will access these *gifts* from our subconscious.

Another way of looking at a *gift* is as a *program.* Everyone by now has owned or had access to some form of smart technology. All of the smart technology comes equipped with *programs.* If you take your smartphone, open the search window and start typing the letter *S* I'm sure some suggested words will begin to appear. Why? Well, because the user has a history of searching words with that letter and because the phone is smart it remembers the history and begins to autofill for the user what it knows or has already learned. The same is true for us as Afrikan people, we have a *history,* and we remember what we have learned. Also true, we begin to *autofill* thinking and behavior patterns from our history (parents and grandparents) into present-day interactions. As we acknowledge our *gifts* and source their origins we create relevant context for our healing journey and can assess if we have moved the needle on debilitating *programs.*

Roles within the family

Family is a sacred space, a space where we construct our identity and formulate schema that we later generalize to other people and experiences. Therefore, the family space has to be protected by all means and with all measures. A broken, hurt, imbalanced, or fragile family system is a breeding environment for dis-ease and fragmentation for black life. Afrikan mothers, fathers, and children have to begin to take note of the manifested social roles and identities produced by wounded family systems. In my work with families and groups, I was exposed to some curriculum that identified common family roles. Throughout my years of therapeutic work, I have found the discussion and identification of these roles with clients to have benefit for individuals as well as the family with regard to insight development. I offer this opportunity to you and your family system to explore these roles to see if you recognize any.

If you have time to sit with a child, ask them what child in the family holds the role of *hero*. The child that is responsible, sports or academic standout, independent, the parents brag about and look to validate their good parenting. If the child is able to identify this person easily, then they are also easily identifying an imbalance in the family system. Next, ask the child who in the family is the *scapegoat*. The child that gets in trouble at school, has anger outbursts, causes problems for the family, and is usually involved with some negative experience. Again if the child can identify the scapegoat, they are validating a kink in the family system. Follow up by asking the child who is the *caretaker*. The child that is the family clown, intervenes in moments of stress with some form of distraction to divert the family's pain or anger. Yes, the caretaker is a needed role within a fragile family system. Finally, ask the child who is the *lost child*. The lost child isolates and may appear to be an emotionally calm person. The lost child daydreams, fantasizes, and appears to have no focus or set direction. If you sit with a child and they can answer these questions with little hesitation and surety, they are speaking to a family system in need of healing. Each of these manifested social roles and identities offers insight and dictates the need for restoration. Let's look briefly at the psycho-social-emotional profiles of each of these roles.

The *hero* has learned to be independent, follow the rules or expectations, follow through on tasks and accomplish things. All of these characteristics are vital to healthy child development, however, the hero has done so to excess. The hero has been over-praised for their accomplishments and success. Over time their experience produces rigid, judgmental and controlling behavior.

The *scapegoat* has learned emotional honesty and attunement to the emotional challenges of the family system. These characteristics are essential to healthy development, however, the scapegoat is also in a state of excess acting out the emotional distress experienced by the family. The scapegoats acting out behavior is met with attention and reinforcement. Over time their experience produces a negative self-image and understanding with a disposition toward seeking negative attention.

The *caretaker* has learned to take responsibility for the emotional well-being of the family. This characteristic is necessary for healthy development, however, the caretaker represents excess as well. The caretaker tries to divert negative family feelings and experiences through humor or other social creations. Over time the caretaker learns to give love but not receive it, they find themselves inefficient at getting their needs met in relationships.

The *lost child* has learned how to self-soothe and be with him/herself. This is a vital characteristic of healthy human development, however, the lost child is a manifestation of skill excess. The lost child self-soothes or rather distracts themselves from reality instead of being present in it. The lost child isolates and denies their feelings in order to create a sense of safety and prevent being hurt.

All of these roles and others are manifestations of imbalanced family systems. Family systems that are deficient in meeting the needs of each individual therefore creating imbalanced character traits. None of these roles are assigned to family members nor are they typically identified or discussed as a family. Instead, these roles and characteristics are developed and acted out day after day after day by members of the family. The daily repetition of having a thought validated by experience and interaction is the construction of *worldview.* Worldview being the confirmed belief of how the world works and how we show up in it. A worldview constructed with imbalance will undoubtedly lead to imbalanced behavior and relationships. And because our families have been the incubator for establishing the imbalanced worldview, our Afrikan children grow into adolescence and adults that seek out imbalanced relationships in other areas of their lives. They seek people and places that will confirm their understanding of the world and how it works. A family member is not limited to holding only one of these roles. Our children may find themselves holding multiple roles of imbalance. As black men, part of our healing is to restore healthy cultural balance to our family systems so that our children may learn, live, and seek balance. We have to establish our homes as the incubation space for healthy balanced thinking and relationship experiences. As we commit ourselves to restoring our family systems, we create opportunities to reconcile our cycles of hurt.

Recycle your pain

I recall as a college athlete my coach asking me the question, ***"Are you hurt or injured?"*** I will never forget those words. In my life, I have applied the intended meaning and principle behind these words to overcome, work through, and reconcile cycles of hurt. My coach never explained his words, but I understood that his reference to *hurt* was about experiencing *pain* and that being *injured* was about not having the capacity or ability to continue. Pain is uncomfortable but temporary and usually an indicator that you are close to success if you press forward. As I learned these lessons, I began training myself to become comfortable being uncomfortable. I began to not only embrace pain and discomfort, but I also I started to search for it, create it, and recycle it. Unlike my coach's words, I had to learn to differentiate *Hurt* from *Pain.* I constructed the understanding that *pain* was simply the sensation (physical, mental, emotional) experienced. While *hurt* was the product or footprint left behind as a result of an unproductive interaction. As a result of this understanding, I concluded that *hurt* has to be *healed* and *pain* is better *recycled*!

A lesson that our Afrikan boys have to understand is that pain is inescapable and must be recycled. They must learn to become familiar with and embrace those physical, mental, and emotional sensations because on the other side of pain is success. As our black boys become acquainted with the process of pain, they can learn to master and recycle those sensations for use at a later time and place. I have never forgotten the sensation (pain) of losing my father. And more than not forgetting, I have stored that pain in a sacred place that I can retrieve it from on demand.

The physical, emotional, and psychological sensations connected to losing my father is also associated with a cycle of hurt. My father did not die at 50, 60 or 70 years old, he died at 38 years of age. A young man whose potential never reached full maturity. Potentials never achieved because he didn't trust himself enough to bet everything on him. Gifts and time never shared with his children because he was engulfed by his own dis-ease. Reverence and support not given to my mother because of value compromise, unhealthy stress responses, and *I* over *We* thinking. These were all unresolved cycles of hurt *gifted* to my father and lived out by him. I know and bear witness that he actively worked at resolving these cycles, however, they were never fully reconciled. Therefore, in the pain of his death are the physical, emotional, and psychological sensations that inform me to press forward. They demand I complete what he was unable, they demand redemption, and they demand reconciliation. Pain has become a fuel to resolve my past, improve my present, and secure my future!

I reflect around four years back sitting with colleagues during supervision. We would always begin with a check-in or update on things we had going on. I remember the look on my peers' faces when I would rattle off my list (full time graduate student, full time employee, contracted work at two organizations, husband, community outreach, starting a business and raising children). We would talk about self-care and making sure we were balancing our priorities. But what I understood was *short term pain long term pleasure!* Pain kept me balanced because it reminded me of my purpose and love. I was working for my last name not my first. I was fulfilling a commitment and repaying a debt to those that I love and those that loved me.

Afrikan men let us not be deterred or discouraged by pain. Let us not be disenchanted or compromised by pain. Let those sensations inform us that we are close to success if we but find the resolve to press forward. Let us press forward in our marriages! Let us press forward in our parenting! Let us press forward in our keeping close family relationships! Let us press forward in building a healthy community! And let us press forward on our quest for healing and wholeness! Recycle your pain and heal your hurts; this is the path of the courageous but more importantly the creed of healing!

PRINCIPLE 3 IN ACTION
Healing/Raising look like

- **Black boys encouraging and supporting black girls**
- **Black men encouraging and supporting black women**
- **Black men zealously involved in the lives of black girls**
- **Black boys obeying and respecting their mother**
- **Black men working through relationship challenges with black women**
- **Black boys completing any task they start with proficiency despite challenges**
- **Black men reflecting on their past and allowing it to inform their present**
- **Black men teaching black boys accountability**
- **Black families attending to the needs of all their children**

"Whatever makes you a man and only you will know what that is, don't ever let anyone cross that line without a response." ~ John Rudell Withers (Told to Kasim age 14)
(Interpreted to mean: Pay attention to how you feel, listen to your gut, interpret what it's telling you to do, then act in accordance pursuing justice).

PRINCIPLE IV
Constructing thoughts for manhood

"You can't miss when you put em through yourself." ~ John Rudell Withers (Told to Kasim age 15)
(Interpreted to mean: You have to invest and believe in yourself even when things get tough. Whatever you are looking to achieve rely on you to get it done.)

Mining our own business

As Afrikan men, we have to practice and teach our sons that Black men *mine* our OWN business. The greatest tragedy and cause of intergenerational dis-ease passed down to black boys and lived out by black men is the absent father. Absenteeism has many variations and presentations that all produce the same result, imbalance. There is the ***physically absent father***. This is the black child that grows without seeing, hearing, touching or interacting with his father's presence. The father has gone off to raise another or someone else's children, has become incarcerated, lives out of the state or country or simply chooses to disengage in parental responsibilities. Then you have the ***emotionally absent father***. This Afrikan child may see, hear, or have the opportunity to touch and interact with his father. However, his father is emotionally restricted or arrested. The father shows a limited range of effect and intensity of emotion during interactions. The father's touch, words, and activity with the child follow a restricted and arrested emotional paradigm. The child believes the father doesn't care, is always angry, or detached from the role of father. I have personally lived out (emotional absence) with my children. Next you have the *financially absent father*. This child rarely experiences the financial support or investment from his father. The father withholds finances based on his emotional disposition, the father is not looked upon as a provider, the father has not adequately positioned himself financially to be a provider. This father is financially irresponsible, he spends on himself and withholds from his children and any money contributed to the life of his child is like pulling teeth without novocaine. Finally, there is the *morally absent father*. This child has not received a moral or ethical code of conduct from his father by which he can use to navigate people and environments. The father demonstrates moral apathy, engages in unethical behavior and presents no moral guide for manhood. All of these forms of absenteeism by black fathers produce deficiency and excess within our Afrikan boys leaving them improperly cultivated. Afrikan men, we have to be *present in order to mine* our business, to cultivate our precious gems, and raise healthy Afrikan successors. I could rest on the importance of black fathers mining the business of our black boys and explain that this book is about black men and boys. However, because of the significant and emotionally destructive impact an absent black father has on the life of our precious black girls, I have to offer an anecdote to bring fullness to the dialogue.

Zoom In

I was working at a middle school on a day I encountered three girls sitting in the main office after being involved in three separate fights. I could overhear the girls bragging and discussing the details of the fights. The dialogue was non-stop; each girl inserting another detail, explaining who did what, when and where it happened. As I warmed some food in the microwave, I leaned out the staff lounge and said, "So, which one of your dads is going to whoop your butt when you get home?" Their respective responses were, *"My dad is in jail." "I don't live with my dad." "I don't have a dad."* The mood shifted from playing and bragging to a quiet pause of reflection. One of the girls immediately said to the other, *"Girl you don't have a dad? I know my dad!"* The girl responded, *"I know who my dad is, he's just never been involved in my life."* The first girl said with conviction, *"Well, my dad he's a good dad. He's tries to pay child support sometimes."* The space again became heavy and quiet. Then one of the girls said to the group, *"Is it bad if I get sad when I think about my dad?"* Afrikan brothers, this is the state that we have left our daughters, abandoned, in need of attention, in hope of reassurance, and deficient in love. In our absence, they have developed with deficiency from neglect. They are acting out their hurt, pain, and lack of self-love by trying to destroy external representations of themselves. Our absence and silence has taught them they are not worthy of love, therefore, they have learned to undervalue and hate themselves. It is the charge of every Afrikan man to mine the business of our precious Afrikan daughters as they are deserving and essential to our healing. We will never be whole so long as the sacred vessel from which we come is harmed, neglected, and unmined. Black men take pride in attending to and cultivating our black girls, they are *the community keepers*!

Black life does not *matter*, Black life is *sacred.* No disrespect to the social movement but the words *Black lives matter* simply does not capture the magnitude nor importance of Afrikan life. Earlier this year, a cinematic action movie was released *Black Panther!* The movie was overwhelmingly received and attended by folks from all walks of humanity. There was a precious mineral in the movie called *Vibranium.* A supernatural, healing, mineral only found in a remote and undisclosed location in Africa. The mineral is so powerful it has to be transported in a special vessel. The mineral has the potential to restore balance to humanity. However, *others* wish to steal the vibranium and use it for evil intent. Again the movie was amazing, great actors, outstanding action scenes, and top of the line graphics. I think many people went to see the movie at least two times. The *Wakanda forever* movement was started February 2018. Black people all around the globe emotionally connected, showed up to the movie premiere in traditional Afrikan garb celebrating black excellence! And yes, I was among the supporters. I truly loved the movie. Yet, I believe that the metaphor presented in the movie and its esoteric meaning escaped the consciousness of many Afrikan people.

Black people, I'll let you in on something, the *Vibranium* is YOU! The Afrikan is the precious mineral with restorative properties. And yes, this precious mineral can only be found in the untapped consciousness of YOUR mind. And yes, vibranium (black children) have to be mined by healthy family and community. Even more important, vibranium has to be transported through a special vessel, the *Afrikan woman.* I know, I know, its deep and you missed it. Black men mining our business is the business of reverence for our Afrikan women that carry our precious (black children) vibranium. Mining our business is being present and attending to the healthy cultivation of our families. The absent black father negatively impacts the unlimited potential of our black children. As we (Afrikan men) move from dis-ease to health and wellness, we must move from absentee behavior to being fully present.

If you examine the nuanced behavior of black dis-ease, you will find a pattern of preoccupation with *past* or *future* thinking. I don't mean reflecting on the past or setting goals for the future. I am speaking to a *stuckness* in the past or distracted *running* toward the future. This is imbalance constructed by absent black fathers. Therefore, Afrikan men, it becomes our political agenda to restore this imbalance and create a healthy construct for black manhood through the practice of (mining our business) being present! We have to be present physically, we have to be present emotionally, we have to be present financially, and we have to be present morally. The action of being present is restorative and wellness producing behavior. To be *present* as a black man is to consciously act in the best interest of the family offering wellness at that specific moment. This is a book about healing and healing is a present moment phenomenon. That means it is happening right now, not in the past or in the future. We don't have to wait on it, we can experience healing right now in the moment. Healing lets us know we are in process and fully present on our journey. So I conclude, black life does not matter it is *sacred* and must be nurtured and cared for in the present moment.

Zoom In

The first jewel of self-worth, self-love, and self-efficacy communicated to me by my father came when I was around seven or eight years old. I came home from school telling my father about the differences between other classmates and me. My father looked me right in my eyes and said, *"You're black and you're Muslim, you are going to be different. You better learn how to love and appreciate yourself. Who wants to be like everyone else anyway!"* That was the end of the conversation. My father had a way of communicating that was so direct that when he finished, you didn't have questions it was just understood. I knew his words meant be comfortable being yourself, accept yourself and seek internal validation rather than making comparisons to "other" people. My father was teaching me to *mind my own business.* In addition to teaching me to mind my business, my father also taught me to *mine my own business.* His words said love and appreciate yourself because you are phenomenal and great. However, it was his actions that gave weight to his words.

In third grade (8 years old) my father came on a school camping trip (camp courage) with me. He ate breakfast with me in the lunchroom that morning before we left on the bus. I recall feeling proud, kids came up to my dad and asked him questions, looked in awe and adults showed him great respect. My father was a people's person and yet genuinely himself. Camp Courage was one of the best experiences in my life. Each day we woke and went on hikes, fished, swam, or canoed; my dad (John Rudell Withers) was a standout! He knew how to do it all, he even knew things my teachers didn't and he was good at translating the information to kids. My dad (a country boy from the south) was the star of the trip, every kid wanted to be in our group for everything. A highlight for us as kids was a day on the basketball court. We were out there playing when the teachers decided to get involved and show their skills. Well, John *the legend* got on the court and destroyed every staff member, shot after shot, move after move, and man, he looked good doing it! I remember him walking off the court smiling and putting his hand on my head and pulling me in close as if to tell me *son see who we are, see what we can do, we are great people.* The last night of Camp Courage everyone met down in the big hall to tell stories and make smores. When I saw all the kids eating smores, I felt left out and began to shy away. My dad looked at me and asked what was wrong. Feeling defeated I said, "*I know we can't eat the smores because the marshmallows have pork in them.*" My dad looked me in the eyes smiling and said, "*Yeah, but we can eat them graham crackers and chocolate!*" We laughed so hard then went right over and grabbed our treats. These fond memories and many others were the deliberate actions by my father to *mine his business*. My father was developing the attitudes, beliefs, work ethic, values, and talents of (his son) his business. The exact skills and talents mined by my father (and of course mother) in my childhood were forged by the pressure of my adolescence and cut through my experiences in young adulthood until they formed me, their business.

Fathers, to mine your business you have to know what you're looking for. You have to understand and discern between precious gems. A ruby has value just as a diamond but they are not cultivated the same, found in the same place, nor assessed by the same measures for quality. To know our children's gifts and spend the time to invest in them is to regularly study and be present with them as they mature into their greatness. We can't get caught in the trap of thinking or wanting all of our black boys to be star athletes, and when they show talent in Math or Art, we shun them or show less enthusiasm. Whatever the talents of our Afrikan children, it is our responsibility to cultivate it to full maturity. That means to guide until full potential is reached and mastery developed. Afrikan children that are developed to their full potential offer a 1,000 percent return on investment to their family and community.

You're not a hustler

In order for black men to be whole, we have to experience financial self-sufficiency and independence. The spirit of entrepreneurship and self-investment has to be a fundamental concept of manhood for black boys. I began my journey of entrepreneurship around my late twenties, however, I was introduced to the idea at age twelve. I was involved in a program called 100 African American Men. The program consisted of one-hundred black (men) entrepreneurs mentoring and working alongside black boys from the community to develop functioning small businesses. I would attend the program on Saturdays all day at Central high school located in St. Paul, Minnesota. These men were teaching us to be proud of our Afrikan heritage, how to be a community, run a business, and rely on ourselves. The entire process was organically constructed. The men sat with us, talked about our homes, community, and Afrikan identity. They gathered our insight and suggestions about what needs we saw in the community and opportunities to earn money. I enjoyed going to the program not because I was overly concerned with business but because the men listened, asked questions, supported our ideas, and most of all, they took us out to eat every meeting! I loved to eat and the men would pay for everything with no problem. We would walk into the local McDonald's or Burger King and people treated us with respect. We carried ourselves with respect, our mentors demanded it. We were maybe a few months into the program when all the mentees were identified and assigned a position in the company. I was assigned the position *VP of finance*. I felt proud to call myself a Vice President. That day, I ran home excited this time more about my position than the food we just ate. I remember, my older brother and dad were in the living room when I arrived. I said to my dad (smiling from ear to ear happy), *"Daddy I'm the VP of finance!"* My dad looked at me and said, *"Oh you're the VP of an ass!"* My dad laughed then my brother. I felt ashamed, put down, discouraged, and humiliated. I never returned to the program. I didn't know it then but later I would understand that my father's words and behavior were a manifestation of his hurt, insecurity, and resentment that other men were pouring into his son in a way that he could not and was not. I felt cheated that I did not have the opportunity to learn the lessons that the 100 African American Men experience could have taught me. However, almost two decades later, I was reintroduced to the lessons by a Black woman.

I had the pleasure of being raised and nurtured by many adults both men and women throughout my life. Of course my biological mother and father but also aunts, uncles, cousins, and community members. One experience that I am forever grateful to have had is being nurtured by (Mrs. Lou Thelma Wiley) my mother-in-law. I don't even like to say, mother-in-law. The way Ms. Wiley mothered me was truly a gift that felt like the love a mother offers to a child she has birthed. I say that without taking anything away from how (Marie Elena Swan) my mother loved, nurtured, and raised me. But rather in complement to the nurturing that my mother offered me.

One particular day sitting in Ms. Wiley's dining room, my wife and I were discussing finances and the challenges of making ends meet. Overhearing the discussion and stepping in as support to her daughter Ms. Wiley said, *"Kasim, you're just not a hustler."* Immediately my wife jumped in defense of me saying, *"wait momma."* I interject,

"Tinaisha, no. Your mother can tell me anything she wants." Ms. Wiley proceeded, *"Kasim, you're the type of guy that just gets up and goes to work, and that's it. See me, I worked and I had my part-time jobs."* I digested every bit of my mother's words, those spoken and those unspoken. Before then I don't recall having any understanding of *hustling* or should I say legal *hustling*. After that day, I would begin to invest in myself, use my creativity, skill-set, and passion to create multiple streams of income. And so the entrepreneur was born.

In the summer of 2011, I took my passion for social justice, consciousness-raising, and empowerment to create the *American Oppressed Race Card*. Creating the race card was my first attempt at implementing basic hustler principles. The name of the game was supply and demand, identify a target audience, assess a need, and then supply a product. I wasn't the type of guy that wanted to become a hustler; I just wanted to understand the art of hustling. What I mean is, a hustler will sell anything that can make a profit. I wanted to learn the skill of making a profit from products and services that would create change.

The *Race Card* was (is) an actual card. On the front, the words *American Oppressed* with the image of a shackled Afrikan. On either side of the Afrikan's image legislation identifying sanctioned (civil rights act, ⅗ compromise) oppression of black people. The card resembled a credit card. The back of the card read *the giver of this card offers you to reflect on one or more of the following.* Below that statement were examples of how racism is expressed during daily interactions. The *Race Card* was (is) a push to identify and change individual and institutional racism (person to person). The actual card was the (social justice), *work* the *hustle* (income stream) was the shirts. I took the imagery of the *Race Card* and placed it on black t-shirts with the words *Raising Social Consciousness.* Then proceeded to sell them at the only place they would be bought in Minnesota, the first Annual Black History Expo. The shirts were a success! Black people came out to a black event and without a lot of explanation understood the powerful imagery and felt the need to declare their support and validate their experience with a $20 purchase. Thank you, (to the late) Ms. Lou Thelma Wiley, for teaching me the art of hustle. The other valuable lesson that I learned and is important for black men and boys to learn is investing in ourselves!

Healthy Stress Responses

Black boys will undoubtedly experience stress growing up, and stress will only increase as their roles and responsibilities increase. Therefore, it is essential to train and teach our Afrikan boys healthy stress responses. An Afrikan boy should never be taught to avoid or attempt to live a stress free life. That concept is antithetical to black manhood and the pathway to greatness. I'm not suggesting that we place on the shoulders of our black boys the *life is hard, be tough* motto. I'm offering the strategic psychological practice of preparing our Afrikan boys to embrace stress and work through it with consciousness. I am proposing a shift in experience for our black boys as they navigate this world to practice ***conscious discomfort*** versus environmentally reactive discomfort. Conscious discomfort is a mindful state of intentionally stress provoking experiences purposed to achieve a desired outcome and build resilience.

Committed sports athletes likely know the concept of conscious discomfort. The child that runs extra sprints after practice to build their endurance. The athlete that weight trains to increase their power and explosion. These and many more are examples of self-imposed discomfort with an intended outcome. Athletes that engage in these forms of self-disciplined practices find themselves at the top of their sport and leaders amongst their peers. More importantly, these athletes have constructed an action-oriented mindset and belief that they possess the ability to inform and influence their future outcomes. Our Afrikan boys have to be trained in a similar fashion with regard to their identities as men.

In order to become healthy Afrikan men, our black boys must learn to navigate stress with healthy behavior and psychology. The first step in building healthy stress responses in our black boys is to reposition their psychology from *I* to *We*. Black boys have to have a political identity that is connected to their cultural worldview of *we* and *us*. An Afrikan boy that understands every decision he makes has to be informed by the question *What is in the best interest of the family/community* is well on his way to developing healthy stress responses. A black boy that is trained to examine the impact of his personal choices on others is learning both empathy and foresight. This teaches black boys to become concerned with communal impact and long-term consequences, which is the psychology of healthy Afrikan manhood. My father used to say it best when he would say, "*Short term pain, long term pleasure!*" The dis-ease that is found in unhealthy stress responses is typically a result in the desire for immediate self-gratification or reduction in present moment pain. Unhealthy stress responses are usually *I* motivated, meaning the thinking and behavior is selfish. Our sports coaches tried to teach the negative consequences of being *I* motivated when they said *There's No I in TEAM!*

The next step in developing healthy stress responses in our Afrikan boys is teaching them to ask for support. Support is not about doing it for them or removing the burden of stress. Support is about cooperation and togetherness to ensure success and remove the sense of overwhelm. Our Afrikan boys have to know that they are never alone in their challenges and that they will receive support when they need it. Again unhealthy stress responses are typically a function of feeling overwhelmed, isolated, and fear of failure. Therefore, it is incumbent upon Afrikan parents and community members to surround our Black boys with healthy and responsive support systems.

The final step in developing healthy stress responses in our black boys is to build distress tolerance skills and their ability to remain in the present moment. Our Afrikan boys have to develop emotional intelligence and capacity. That means the ability to accurately identify emotions, understand what they are telling them to do and the endurance to experience the emotion from beginning to end. This is what is meant by distress tolerance and being in the present moment. Unhealthy stress responses typically have an element of avoidance and distraction attached to them. The avoidance is usually about fear of (the future) what is to come. *I can't handle what's about to happen, so I will find a way to avoid it.* Distraction is commonly connected to the lack of capacity to work through the emotional intensity of an experience. *This is too much to sit with, so I will find something to take my attention away from it.* Distress tolerance allows us to ride the emotional wave through its (greatest intensity) peek and come to a successful finishing point. Learning to remain present allows us to remove the fear of the unknown and replace it with acceptance of the here and now.

I learned the concept of healthy stress responses in early adolescence watching my older peers navigate life. I was an observer of human nature at an early age. I was constantly trying to figure out why people did what they did and what motivated them to do so. I used the experiences of others to inform my behavior. I grew up in an environment where weakness was exploited and strength worshiped. I wanted to transform myself into the strongest version of myself possible. So as a teenager I watched my peers drink alcohol. I asked myself the question, *"What is the motivation and what is the gain?"* What I found was that most of my peers drank to avoid or distract. I noticed that some folks needed a drink to be social. They were trying to avoid social awkwardness. Others were drinking to distract themselves from current responsibilities or problems. I use to say to myself, *"They have to drink to talk to girls, they have to drink to get through life. Naw I'm good. I'm stronger than that."* As a result, I built some pretty healthy stress responses. I didn't succumb to alcohol, drugs, gambling or extreme violence as a stress response. I made exercise, prayer, reflection, optimism, and routine my stress responses. These responses were healthy, beneficial, and produced resilience. Now, I have to be honest, I also developed a few unhealthy stress responses that just like I mentioned earlier were steeped in distraction and avoidance. These responses would later have to be worked on and removed from my choices of how to respond to stress. I have made tremendous progress in this area and I'm still on my journey. However, my main strategy for developing my responses to stress were observing peers and critiquing their outcomes as well as motivations. It is necessary that Afrikan boys learn and implement this cognitive-behavioral process, their health is contingent upon it.

Necessary but not a Guarantee

A mandatory concept that has to be confirmed upon the minds and hearts of Afrikan boys is that *Manhood is necessary, but it is not a guarantee.* I mean our black boys have to understand that within them is the potential to become men, however, that potential is not miraculously activated when they turn eighteen or twenty-five. Black boys hear me clearly, potential has to be activated and potential left untapped dwindles and dies. Afrikan boys your welcome to manhood comes with a set of conditions, responsibilities, and acquired skills. More importantly, your journey to manhood comes about through shifting your physical and psychological posture.

A serious concept for Afrikan manhood is the evolution of *male posture*. I love and revere the legacy and wisdom that our elder Dr. Na'Im Akbar left us in his writings particularly *Visions for black men*. He offers us a framework to understand steps necessary for transformation from *male, to boy, to man!* My articulation of *male posture* is birthed from his writings and framework. Afrikan boys, you must be taught to evaluate and refine your posture. In infancy, black males are completely dependent thus their posture reflects a *do for me* stance. Black males (infants) look to have their every need met by a caretaker, feed me, clothe me, change me, comfort me, wash me, house me, and do these things IMMEDIATELY! The infant posture is about immediacy and constant request. At this stage of *maleness*, the posture is appropriate. However, to become a boy and eventually a man, this posture has to change. Afrikan boys, it is mandatory to develop and practice *self-discipline and self-determination* as part of your manhood training. A failure to do so will result in *Arrested Development.* That is to say, you will remain stuck in *maleness or boyhood* despite your chronological age or physical stature. I mean, you will have the appearance of a man but still the psychological posture of a *male or a boy*.

It is easy to discern the appropriateness of male posture during infancy as opposed to during teen or adult years.

The infant child asking for their needs to be met is just that, a reasonable and appropriate request based on ability. The teenage boy or adult black male acting with this same posture is no longer making a reasonable or appropriate request, they are BEGGING! This is a serious problem that requires immediate correction. And it has become commonplace as well as accepted by the community. We see it far too often; the black teenager on the corner begging for a cigarette, then your lighter. The adult black male begging for housing, a job, respect, etc. This is not the posture of an Afrikan man. And we have to train our black boys early to have an extreme aversion and distaste for this inappropriate posture. The words spoken by our cultural hero is correct, "*I would rather die on my feet than to live on my knees.*" Many of us are walking around with bloodstained knees, sore backs, and strained necks from begging so much. And I'm not just talking about the brothas hanging out on the street corners. I'm talking about some of the brothas wearing nice suits making good salaries but still bent knee, bowed head begging. The posture of black manhood is strong, erect, self-determined, and executing power with political Afrikan intent!

Zoom In

It doesn't matter where you find yourself as a black man, you have to constantly find opportunities to reach our black boys and train them for manhood. Teach them the posture of self-discipline, self-determination, and Afrikan politics. Trust me there is no greater reward than empowering our black boys with these opportunities to be fathered and trained in becoming men.

I had an experience with a young man that I will never forget, and I'm sure he will never forget either. I knew this child for several years through work experiences. I had the opportunity to know him in early childhood and throughout his teen years. When he was about ten years old, I got a call from my wife saying, *"I have two boys here asking me to buy them food or give them money. They say they know you."* I asked my wife, *"What're their names?"* She only gave me one name and said the other boy won't say. I let her know that I do know the child and to get them whatever they need. Now, this encounter was truly a coincidence. The child had never met my wife, and she didn't know him. The black boy was up in a shopping center begging and happened upon my loving wife who probably interrogated him better than the police to try and figure out his story.

I later had the opportunity to work with this black boy again from eleven to thirteen years old. I don't know what it was but this black boy would ask me almost every week for something. *"I need shoes, I need a haircut, I need pants, give me some food, give me money for a field trip."* On and on and on. I was shocked how much he asked considering I rarely responded with yes to any of his requests. One day, the little brother came to me and asked, *"Why don't you ever get me stuff like I see you doing for everyone else?"* I looked him in his eyes and without blinking told him, *"I'm never going to give you anything!"* I said, *"Little brother, I have a son younger than you and I don't let him ask me for certain things anymore. He has a business and when he wants something he goes out and takes care of business to get what he wants.*" The black boy looked at me and said, "*Yeah, but your son has a dad.*" I wasn't going for it, I laughed and said, "*What do you think I'm here for? Are you ready to be fathered?*" I told him, "*Today we are going to see if you are a fisherman or if you just like to eat fish!*" He said, "*What do you mean?*" I explained, "*A fisherman knows how to go out and get fish to eat. A person who just likes to eat fish is always looking for someone to bring it to them.*" I gave the little brother ten dollars and said, "*If you're a fisherman, tomorrow you will come back with twenty. But if you just like to eat fish, tomorrow you will be broke.*" After that, I gave the little brother a crash course in hustling, examining the wants of people and using it to make a profit. The next day, our black boy approached me with nineteen dollars and a backpack with the last of his inventory (pokemon cards, candy and chewing gum). He actually tried to sell some to me Hahaha. I continued his lesson by explaining profit and reinvestment. In a few days, I saw this young man that typically looked disheveled and in a begging posture walking tall, proud, and strong (fresh haircut, clean clothes, and washed face). I asked him about the haircut. He let me know he paid to go get it cut with his own money. I asked him how it felt, he gave me the biggest smile ever and said, "*It feels good!*" I looked at him and said, "*I'm proud of you, you're a fisherman!*" A ten dollar lesson is all it takes to reconstruct male posture in black boys to an appropriate manhood training posture. This is the work of Afrikan men and a vital concept to teach black boys regarding black manhood. The lessons offered in that short encounter if understood by that black child will serve him forever and create a point of reference to begin to refine as he continues his journey to becoming an Afrikan man. He will forever have an experience of exercising his potential and self-determining outcomes in his life. This is the correct posture of a black man.

A Tool Not A Solution

Given the unrelenting attack on black life, it is vital to have a concept for black manhood that offers *resilience as a tool, not a solution.* I offer this concept and hope that it is understood and practiced with diligence. Afrikan people, we are renowned for our *resilience or grit,* and yet we have to understand that it is a tool, not a solution. Resilience is internal conditioning that allows us to recover or bounce back from difficult external events known as *Life!* I emphasize **Bounce Back** because that is exactly what is happening. We are being stretched to capacity then flung forward forcefully and finally halted abruptly in an attempt to regain our previous form. The process is jarring, and the return to the previous form is not completely possible. Every resilience bout is like pulling back on a rubber band as far as it can stretch then letting it fly. When you go pick that rubber band up, it's not the same, and over time it wears, and eventually, it snaps.

Growing up as a black boy with three black sisters I saw this phenomenon happen at least once or twice a week. I would watch my sisters get their hair done, my mother pulling their hair back, brushing it up, combing to the side then putting on rubber bands. It would never fail, my mother would be working with speed and precision getting their hair together. She always had my sisters between her legs, and they would be holding the rubber bands as she worked. You never knew when it was going to happen but eventually POP! A rubber band would snap. You could tell it was a shock because my sisters would jump slightly and my mother would say, *"Dang it, give me another one."* Resilience is like a rubber band. Resilience has to first be developed then used in complement with other tools and resources. I look around at some of our black boys, and by age fifteen they have already pulled back on their resilience rubber band so many times that you can see the wear and tear on their faces. They are one life experience away from experiencing the **POP!** Resilience is a tool not a solution.

I recall attending a graduate course, and a guest speaker came in to discuss effective teaching strategies. The speaker made an excellent point that speaks to the importance of this concept for black manhood. He said, *"I've worked in the cities and I've worked in the suburbs. The kids in the city are resilient; they have grit, but they lack good support systems. The kids in the suburbs lack grit, but they have excellent support systems.* The speaker was validating the necessary component of healthy family and community support in the lives of black children. He also implied that resilience by itself is insufficient as a solution for Afrikan children. Resilience is not an unlimited commodity to be used for every situation over and over and over again. Resilience is for those life challenges that after receiving family support, community support and you still need that extra piece to bring you through it. Therefore, resilience is a tool, not a solution. Healthy family and healthy community are the solution. Healthy family and healthy community will ensure that resilience is fostered, used strategically and with balance.

As a licensed psychotherapist, I've heard too many stories of resilience rubber bands being pulled back over and over and over again due to lack of family and community support. The result is, *"I don't know if I can do this anymore. I don't want to be here anymore. I tried to overdose this weekend."* Sometimes in our families or communities, we hear these things and create false narratives that these people have a lack of resilience. We pathologize them as being weak and without courage. This is often the furthest thing from the truth. Their condition is caused by overuse of a tool believed to be a solution. Afrikan men, the health of our family and community is vital. We must prioritize our efforts and focus with that in mind. We must build concepts of Afrikan manhood that identify resilience as a tool and healthy family and community as the solution. If we understand, practice, and teach this concept, we will demonstrate with conviction the rebuilding and protection of our (family and community) *sacred spaces* and prevent the overuse of resilience as a means to cope. We will have reconstructed the social-political spaces necessary to heal and thrive. Our charge and mission is healthy Afrikan family and healthy Black communities. Let us not rest until we achieve collective success!

PRINCIPLE 4 IN ACTION
Healing/Raising look like

- Black men studying and accepting their son's for who they are not who they want them to be
- Black men actively developing the talents of black boys
- Black men prioritizing black family and black community as their top priority
- Black boys going through formal rites of passage trainings
- Black men and black boys developing small businesses
- Black boys choosing exercise, prayer, meditation, etc over drug use, violence, alcohol and having sex
- Black families develop a strong support systems for black children
- Black men being present and attending to their family responsibilities

PRINCIPLE V
Finding our complement

"You have to know your personnel." ~ Kasim age 17
(Interpreted to mean: your relationship with others should be based on
having true and accepting the knowledge of who the other person is.
Therefore, your expectations and actions will be met with success).

Complementarity

Black men, a significant principle for establishing balance and wholeness is finding our complement. Finding our complement is a process of self-discovery as well as self-restraint, selectivity, and reciprocation. Our complement is uniquely qualified to bring us into a correct understanding of our purpose as we are likewise for them. In order to find our complement, we must first respond to the sacred wisdom that commands us to *Know thyself.* Knowledge of self is more than knowing your likes and dislikes or your needs and wants. Knowledge of self is knowing your unique gifts and how they can be paired with someone else's unique gifts to create harmony, symmetry, and justice in the world. Additionally, knowledge of self is an appreciation for the shortcomings of self and others as they provide the context for human interaction, which is need, assistance, and support. This is the natural psychology and behavior of human beings (to be communal). Afrikan culture is a communal culture, a natural culture that adheres to balance and justice through a collective *we.* Therefore, finding our complement and knowing thyself is a process and practice of realigning the psychological disposition of Afrikan men to a communal interdependent mode of operation. This psychological realignment is the difference in finding our complement or finding our opposite.

In western culture, there is a common saying that *opposites attract*. Some of you may think that opposites and complements are one in the same. Absolutely not, each of these concepts is steeped in a cultural paradigm and understanding that is eventually acted out through behavior. An insidious characteristic of the *law of opposites* is hierarchical value placement a western cultural paradigm. It adheres to the psychology of rank order or stratification valuing one thing over another. The *law of complements* is a communal paradigm it subscribes to the psychology of interconnectedness. The law of complement does not rank order or place hierarchical value of one thing over another. Even better it does not place one person over another. It acknowledges uniqueness as strength and support for a collective purpose. Each person offering something necessary and equally valuable that completes the collective agenda.

The law of opposites is acted out every day in the United States. The law of opposites or differences can be found in every facet of human life demarcated by data that highlights *racial stratification* or rank-ordered outcomes based on value placement. In the current decade, you see organizations and people attempting to respond to this psychological dis-ease through efforts commonly referred to as *diversity and inclusion work*. These are attempts by organizations to shift the social climate and culture from acting out the psychology of *opposites* to embracing the ideology of *complementarity*. The pervasive sickness connected to the psychological disposition of the law of opposites has penetrated the hearts and minds of Afrikan men and boys. The dis-ease has left us finding our opposites instead of our complements. The shift in our cognition is so subtle and ingrained that it is often overlooked until its debilitating effects begin to attack the family system.

Zoom In

I recall witnessing this thinking as I sat with a new couple preparing to be married. I had the couple complete a premarital survey as common practice to gain insight on thinking patterns as well as obtain background information. As the couple reviewed and shared their answers to the questions with each other, they arrived at a particular question, *"If you could change one thing about your partner what would it be?"* This is a question that speaks to more than the surface level inquiry. The question is identifying values, attitudes, and beliefs. The sista went first and shared her response. The brotha followed behind her with his. This wonderful Afrikan brotha said, *"I truly love everything about her but if there was one thing I could change it would be that she can be indecisive."* The sista even agreed with him. The brotha continued, *"See me I'm decisive, I like to get things done and when I make a decision I follow through on it."* Okay, this isn't beat up on the brotha time, however, this anecdote allows us opportunity to analyze and reflect upon the subtle psychological nuances that impact our cultural health and family dynamic as Afrikan people. I asked the brotha to explain the behavior that the sista does that is indecisive. He began to explain how she will go back and forth on things, change her mind after appearing to decide on something, and take long periods of time before actually committing to a decision and carrying out action. I asked the brotha, *"Okay, explain to me why this is a problem?"* His simple answer was, *"Because I don't do it that way, I make decisions quickly and follow up with actions to get things done, I'm efficient."* This thinking pattern adheres perfectly to the psychology *of opposites.* He has assigned greater value to his unique characteristic and behavior i.e. being efficient is better. Furthermore, his articulation of her behavior was covered in judgment. I offered him the opportunity to reframe his characterization using a *complementarity* lens valuing unique difference for the collective agenda. I said, *"So she considers multiple perspectives and takes her time before making a decision or carrying out action. Has that ever been useful?"* Of course it was easy for the brotha to find examples of when those unique characteristics were of benefit not only to her but to them! I offered the couple the psychological and behavioral practice of *complementarity* when I said to them, *"Our problems are typically a manifestation of thinking and if we can shift our thinking, we can change problems to assets and solutions."* In all honesty, I was only able to offer this insight and so clearly connect to the brotha's thinking because of my own experience with this particular dis-ease. For many years, I was married to my *opposite.* I underappreciated and placed value over the unique characteristics of my wife, often finding myself annoyed and frustrated by her behavior. More importantly, I minimized and failed to acknowledge when her uniqueness benefited me individually and the family collectively. This form of dis-ease was a direct consequence of my socially constructed disposition adhering to the pathological law of opposites.

As we identify and accept (our natural state) who we are, it becomes a demand on our spirit to seek that which will complete us. Finding our complement is discriminatory behavior, it is political behavior, and it is behavior that absolutely requires restraint. Our complements are not an easy fit, however, they are a perfect fit. As stated by a famous actor, *"Ease is a greater threat to success than hardship."* Brothas, finding a partner that will complete you may not be easy, and keeping and healing with that partner will come with hardships. It is in times of hardship that we have the opportunity to show our best stuff, to offer healing and restrain ourselves from seeking the comfort of dis-ease. Hardships produce the circumstances and emotional backdrop to facilitate the experiences necessary for our partners and self to heal. I have been fortunate to not only have a spouse that introduced me to new psychological concepts; but who was also patient as I've learned to translate these new thoughts into new actions.

Zoom Out

At my practice and three other cultural organizations that I had the opportunity to either work as a therapist or clinical supervisor, (at least) eighty-five percent of the clients were female. Additionally, ninety percent of males receiving therapy were brought in, referred, or encouraged to participate in therapy by a female. This is glaring information that speaks to both conceptual imbalance as well as conceptual healing dynamics for black people. As Afrikan people, we have to attend to the pattern of imbalance that Afrikan women and girls (in general) are seeking help sooner and in greater numbers than Afrikan men and boys. If there is truth in this pattern, then we can extrapolate from it that (in general) our homes and communities mirror this pattern of imbalance. Therefore, we should be informed that there is great urgency for black men and boys to seek support and begin healing as a means to restore balance. As it relates to conceptual healing, we can take from this information that black women are vital to the healing process of black men and boys. Our Afrikan women are the dynamo for our healing and restoration from our dis-eased social conditioning. After society has told us that seeking help is not masculine and to need others is weak, our *community keepers* have offered us humanity by bringing us into spaces where we can heal. Our black sisters and mothers are inviting us to be healed and whole so that they may in return experience healing and wholeness. Therefore, we must understand without equivocation *that there is no healing the Afrikan man without healing the Afrikan woman!*

A Love Story

I was introduced to the language of *complementarity* by my wife (Tinaisha Abdur Razzaq), a woman that is truly my complement. She learned the concept from reading Mwalimu K. Bomani Baruti's book *Complementarity: Thoughts for Afrikan Warrior Couples.* Complementarity is about wholeness, being complete, unique apart, and purposeful together. My wife has always been a source of my growth and development sometimes by finesse and others by force! A quote and reminder that my wife has said to me about our complementarity is, *"Don't you understand why in Islam they say marriage is half of your (Deen) way of life? It's because you need me and I need you to complete our purpose!"* My wife is a gem that embodies the true wisdom and spirit of Afrikan womanhood (The community keeper). Another jewel she gave me one day while sitting outside our home on a beautiful day was, *"Kasim you are not strong the way I am strong, and I am not strong the way you are strong. We each have a strength that is needed by the other person, and we have to embrace that truth."* Wheeeew, a young woman with the sage of our great ancestry. Those particular words that day spoke to me and fortified my understanding of complementarity. Her words eloquent and concise resonated within me as I had experienced the fruit of those words throughout our years together. I can recall many an incident needing and calling upon her strength and feeling relief, awe, and gratitude in her abilities. However, if I am completely honest, I have to admit that in those moments my gratitude and awe were not reverence of her unique qualities but more (selfish) appreciation and amazement that I did not have to shoulder the burden of stress. Only today can I say that I have started the shift of having authentic reverence for her strength as an Afrikan woman and the complement that we share together. And yes, I'm still working on it!

On my journey of healing and restoration, I have learned the power of complement experientially. I first began to exercise the wisdom within myself. I knew I was not the man I could be, should be or wanted to be, which meant I had to begin the process of self-work. I went back to an adolescent sports point of reference shared with me by my father, *"If you want to make a drastic improvement in your game in a short period, you have to identify the weakest part of your game and work on that intensely until it becomes a strength."* Thank you, daddy! My father was speaking to complement and balance. As an adult, I implemented this philosophy in an effort to become a better balanced me. I had to take a serious look in the mirror and see my vulnerable areas. It would just so happen that my areas of deficiency were connected to my area of excess (complementing ideas).

As a teenager, I used structure, rigid adherence to time, and self-dependence to bring myself out of circumstantial trauma. Those exact skills over time became tools used in excess, so much so that I had become a rigid time intolerant person (unappreciative of cultural orientation to time). In identifying the excess of rigid behavior, I was able to clearly see its complement, (flexibility) which was my deficient area and area to begin self-work. It would just so happen that flexibility, vision, imagination, and togetherness were the strengths of my wife. That is to say, the lessons I needed to learn were held within my choice of a life-partner. How did I get so lucky to find a partner that held the keys to my humanity and wholeness? Well, I'll start by going back.

At fifteen or sixteen years old, I recall saying to myself, *"I'm not going to marry a woman like my mother."* I loved my mother, but I definitely didn't want the heavy-handed, run and play with the boys, body-slamming people, and whooping neighborhood kids with a switch kind of woman for my wife. My mother (Marie Elena Swan) was all of these things and of course much, much more. Looking back on my childhood with a lens of complementarity, I now see a much broader picture of not only my mother but the relational dynamic between her and my father. As their best selves, they were true complements. My father was a visionary and social-architect. He could mastermind a plan, articulate behavior, and position people for action. My father was a cognitive guru. My mother was an organizer, task-oriented, and morally convicted practitioner. My mother's actions told her story. If she said she loved you, her actions had already beat her mouth to the point. My mother was the queen of execution. In these ways and so many more, my parents complemented each other. And when they were both at their best, they offered wholeness to one another and created childhood experiences for me that were health-producing.

Meeting a complement is simple, the law of attraction will bring you into proximity with people who need what you have to offer. However, the journey to finding *your* complement, that particular person holding unique formula to complete you begins with an authentic understanding of *self. Finding our complement* is the process of searching our mind and spirit for any cultural dis-ease and restoring those spaces with healthy psychology and emotionality that affirms our natural state of being. I mentioned that in my adolescence I affirmed I would never marry a woman like my mother. The woman I found and chose to marry at 22 years old couldn't have been further from my mother with the exception of being a black woman. I was looking for someone *opposite* of my mother. The law of attraction introduced me to my complement, however, I was determined for her to be my *opposite*. I remember three distinct encounters with my wife as an adolescent.

The first time I met my wife was around fifteen years old. I was at the Martin Luther King center shooting ball in an almost empty gym. There was a "woman" with a young child on the other end of the gym, jean skirt, flats, blue top, and purse across her shoulders showing her son how to shoot the ball. I looked over on that side of the court a few times. I thought the woman was beautiful, elegant, and regal. I would later learn the woman was a girl and the boy was her nephew.

The second time I met my wife was my senior year of high school, a new girl being escorted through the halls wearing a cheerleading skirt with soft bouncing hair, exquisite facial features, mocha skin, curvy shape, and graceful presence. I took a shot to introduce myself (huge smile), *"Who is this?"* A staff person said, *"Tinaisha, she is new here from another school."* I responded, *"Well, let me show her around because this is my school."* The staff countered, *"No, you will not be showing her anything."* Later that year, Tinaisha would interview me for snow daze king, and we would take a picture together as royal court. We spoke one other time that year that I can recall, outside the main office after school. We were teenage kids discussing *life* one of the only conversations with a female peer that I ever had where I was completely enthralled.

The third time I met my wife was in a club (the Qwest); I was around nineteen years old. I saw her and some of her friends across the room. I approached with my friends said hello to everyone. A beautiful black woman in a little black dress. I hugged her, and she said, *"Why you hugging me like that? I remember in high school there was a long line of girls trying to talk to you."* I could hear the playful yet serious tone in her voice. My only reply was, *"Well, you right at the front of the line now."* I never saw or heard from her again. Each one of my encounters with Tinaisha from fifteen to nineteen was a soul-touch. Yes, she was attractive, yes graceful, yes eloquent, yes down to earth, but for me, she was a standard. I recognized an authentic connection between she and me that never went away. I knew we fit together.

At twenty-one years old, I was in search of wholeness. I asked my younger sister (Wazira) of Tinaisha's whereabouts. I was informed that she was a student and member of the Orchesis dance company at Grambling State University. *"Wazira will you get her number for me?"* A few weeks later I got a call, *"Hello, yes, is this Kasim? Yes, this is Tinaisha! Why did you ask for my number?"* Four hours later on the phone I was reconnected to wholeness. We continued talking on the phone across states for an entire year. An unexpected car crash that hospitalized Tinaisha and totaled her car brought her back to Minnesota mid-Fall for a new vehicle. She didn't tell me she was in town. I saw her at football game. Her nephew was playing against my youngest brother. I tell you complementarity can improve your vision because that day I saw her across the field in a crowd full of people without my glasses on. Hahaha, yeah, she stood out in the crowd! I walked over and asked if she would come over for dinner later, she agreed. I knew I had one chance that wouldn't come around again and I took it. I said to her, *"I don't do the boyfriend/girlfriend thing. My intention is to marry you!"* We were looking in each other's eyes then she smiled and said, *"Okay."* We continued talking over the phone and across states that year. I came down that summer, met her grandparents and the rest of the family during her college graduation in Louisiana. We drove back to Minnesota together and were married in July 2002. A true love story. My wife tells me all the time, *"The way we met and how everything happened was so beautiful it almost seems surreal!"* I was on my best behavior that year and couldn't have been happier as a person! I had found exactly what I was looking for but hadn't yet found myself.

Building Healthy Family

Building a family takes time, strategy, and work. And to build a healthy Afrikan family takes more than that. It takes healthy community support, political activation, self-refinement, and healing. I am of the opinion that the most revolutionary actions that black people can participate in today are building and maintaining healthy black families and communities. In fact, I'm sure this has to be at the top of our collective priority list if we are to be successful.

The afrikan family is a system that develops the emotional, psychological, and behavioral patterns of our Afrikan children. Therefore, the family system can either nurture or corrupt the health and wholeness of our children. In order to raise healthy black boys, they must be raised in a healthy family system. A healthy black family system nurtures the value of collectivism, the behavior of being responsible, the feeling of accountability, and the architecture of *Healthy circuitry*. Circuitry is a vital component and pillar that healthy Afrikan families must be built upon.

Healthy circuitry is a system of free flowing reciprocal energy/effort that produces politically positive outcomes for every participant in the circuit. To have circuitry in our families, every member has to make a complementary contribution. Complementary contributions ensure a reciprocal give and take process throughout the family that helps to build it up and replenish its resources. A black family with healthy circuitry is cooperative, self-protective, and self-sustaining. Although *healthy circuitry* is the ideal state of the Afrikan family, many of our families are suffering from *broken circuitry*.

Broken Circuitry is a system of unilaterally flowing energy/effort that has a linear start and end point, which produces politically deficient outcomes. Broken circuitry has a non-reciprocal give and take process where only some members of the circuit experience positive outcomes. This is a family system that becomes debilitated over time inhibiting its ability to self-protect or self-sustain. Broken circuitry is most commonly seen in families where black women shoulder disproportionate care and responsibility for the family system. This is a dynamic that can be seen in both single parent homes as well as two-parent homes. The dynamic of Afrikan women left to attend to the spiritual, educational, moral, social, physical, financial, emotional, nutritional, and psychological development of the family. Our black women have carried out these family functions for the most part without reprieve or reciprocation. The end result is extreme fatigue and debilitated wellness for our Afrikan mothers.

My mother and father can be counted among the Afrikan children that experienced the impact of broken circuitry in their family systems. They can also be mentioned with black parents who practiced unilaterally flowing energy/effort that did not reciprocate. Over two decades, I observed my mother give it all and get very little in return. From booster clubs, school field trips, enrichment, academics, religion, character development, sports, and social life, my mother was there for it all. I became so used to having her constant flow of energy that I became embarrassed, unappreciative, and non-reciprocal. I used to kiss my mother every night, massage her feet, walk on her back, cook with her, and go grocery shopping with her to reciprocate healthy circuitry. But over time I began to neglect my responsibility, I became a taker. I assisted in creating broken circuitry.

Building a healthy Afrikan family dictates that black boys and black men connect willingly and completely to the circuitry of the family. Our black boys have to learn and practice cooperative support with their sisters and girls in the community. Likewise, black men have to demonstrate this committed practice with our spouses and sisters (those with kinship ties and those without). In doing so, we have to understand that our cooperation won't look equal but it will feel replenishing. Again healthy Afrkan psychology accepts that our contributions be complementary not be the same because we seek wholeness, not fragmented equality. Building a healthy black family, the politics will always be *We* and the circuitry free flowing and reciprocal.

From deficiency & Excess to balance

We live in a time of **product** excess and **process** deficiency. As Afrikan people, this paradigm is at the crux of our hurt and disequilibrium. Our love and excitement to celebrate *products* have overshadowed our cultural values and attention to *process*. We have become obsessed with *products* like winning instead of *processes* like doing our best. The result of these excessive and deficient practices has left black men and boys feeling unworthy.

Many Afrikan men and boys today walk around with thoughts and feelings of not being worthy. We feel unworthy of love, unworthy of leadership, unworthy of respect, unworthy of trust, and unworthy of honor. As a result, we have placed our value of *self* in our ability to obtain and show to others that we have acquired *products* as a means of proving our **worth!** This internal conflict has formed our dispositions of either excess (obsessed with accomplishments) or deficiency (lack of will and motivation to try). Additionally, our internal turmoil has placed us in a hyper-competitive psychological state. We assess and value ourselves through comparisons with others trying to best someone else's accomplishments or achieved social status. This is a culturally deficient psychological state that produces megalomania and destruction of our collective Afrikan agenda.

I know the consequences of this psychological state all too well. I testify that excess and deficiency are both *products* of unbalanced *process.* Throughout more than fifteen years of marriage, I learned that I could accomplish pretty much whatever I set my focus on. However, in the past two years, I was taught that product could not be valued over process. Instead, they have to work in complement and harmony with one another. The harmony of *process* and *product* is achieved through *balance.* Balance is both an achievable state as well as something to strive toward. Therefore, balance is the synergy of process and product. It is an ongoing journey with moments of accomplished celebration. Balance teaches us to be attentive, to refine, and to persist finding a middle road. *What is it for a man to gain the whole world but lose his own soul?*

Afrikan men, we have to shift our thinking and behavior to living balanced and having balanced relationships. We must actively work to resolve dynamics that have conditioned us to internalize the lie that being fallible or in the process of healing makes us unworthy of our humanity. Furthermore, we have to rid ourselves of dis-eased psychology that has us in a state of perpetual competition. As we learn to reconstruct our thoughts and behavior to coincide with our cultural values, we prepare ourselves for harmony and balance with our partners. We become capable of offering them justice and their mutual right of complementarity. Until we do so, we will continue to foster unhealthy relationships acting with a spirit of *arrested development* and immaturity. Our imbalance will never allow us to find our complement, it will only offer us an opposite.

I am overjoyed to say that I am healing; as a black man, I am not there, but I am in the process. I am finding opportunity to acknowledge where I am in the present and choose actions that realign my past in order to create a healthy future. Healing is uncomfortable, healing is vulnerable, healing is hard work, and healing is wonderful! As I continue to engage my healing, I am beginning to *find my complement* and reinterpret my past. The thoughts I had as a hurt and imbalanced teen that said, "*I will never marry my mom,*" now have informed meaning. Through my healing, I have learned that those words were intended to be, "*I will never allow my wife to hurt like my mother.*" If I am ever to be true to these words, then my commitment has to be healing.

A part of my healing has been accepting that not only did I marry my mother, but I intentionally and zealously searched for her. The mother that I could be vulnerable with; the mother I felt deep emotional connection to; the mother I was protective of; the mother that nurtured me; the mother that held me accountable; the mother I revered, and the mother that nursed me to wellness. My black mother was my first teacher of healing. May the most high accept her deeds and reward her with the highest level of paradise.

To heal is to return to our natural state, which denotes revisiting our past. My beloved wife is a visit to my past. I mean truly a visit back to my (*essence*) mother. The lives of my wife and mother parallel in so many ways I couldn't have consciously known. They share the same birth month, private Catholic school upbringing, Tom-boys, extrovert personality, and unwavering loyalty. My wife's attributes are reconnecting me to my past and offering me the opportunity to return to my natural state. I am learning deep emotional connection, I am learning to be protective, I am learning to revere, and I am learning to be vulnerable.

Afrikan men I remind you as I remind myself, we are not healed, we are healing. Let us become immortalized in the present moment of our responsibilities. Let us reconstruct our psychology to the collective *We.* Let us find our complements and never allow them to become our opposites. Let us be balanced, let us be healthy, let us be complete, let us be restored. And how will we know when we get there? How will we know when we have found our complement? How will we know when we have transitioned through our dis-ease? We will know because we will live out our ancient cultural practice of *Nation building!* Not on the backs of our Afrikan women, not at the expense of our Afrikan children, and not through the exploitation of our Afrikan community. But we will *Nation build* with our Black women, for our Black children, and to the benefit of our Black community. So let it be written, so let it be done!

PRINCIPLE 5 IN ACTION
Healing looks like

- **Black men finding their worth in establishing healthy black families and communities**
- **Black boys engaging in cooperative play and projects with black girls**
- **Black men and black women supporting each other in building institutions together**
- **Black men developing a communal psychology and appreciation for uniqueness**
- **Black men supporting each other in their work with a spirit of togetherness**
- **Black boys placing value on doing their best**
- **Black men and boys seeking early intervention and support**

Bibliography

Akbar, N. (1991, 2000). Vision for Black Men. Tallahassee, FL: Mind Productions and Associates.

Akbar, N. (1999). Know Thy Self. Tallahassee, FL: Mind Productions and Associates.

Akbar, N. (1996, 1999). Breaking The Chains of Psychological Slavery. Tallahassee, FL: Mind Productions and Associates.

Ani, M. (1994). Yurugu: An African-Centered Critique of European Cultural Thought and Behavior. Trenton, NJ: African World Press.

Carbado, D.W. & Gulati, M. (2013). Acting White: Rethinking Race in "Post Racial" America. New York, NY: Oxford Press University

Hamilton, C.V. & Ture, K. (1967). Black Power: The Politics of Liberation. NY: Random House.

Kunjufu, J. (2005). Countering the Conspiracy to Destroy Black Boys. Chicago, IL: African American Images.

Wilson, A.N. (1993). The Falsification of Afrikan Consciousness. Bronx, NY: Afrikan World Infosystems.

Woodson, C.G. (1933, 1990). The Miseducation of the Negro. Trenton, NJ: Africa World Press, Inc.

Wright, B. (1986). "The Psychopathic Racial Personality." Chicago: Third World Press.